1 0 S T E P S T O

Successful Business Alignment

1 0 STEPS TO

Successful
Business
Alignment

Patricia Pulliam Phillips & Jack J. Phillips

ASTD Press is an internationally renowned source of insightful and practical information on workplace learning and performance topics, including training ba-sics, evaluation and return-on-investment, instructional systems development, e-learning, leadership, and career development.

Ordering information: Books published by ASTD Press can be purchased by visiting ASTD's website at store.astd.org or by calling 800.628.2783 or 703.683.8100.

Library of Congress Control Number: 2011944558
ISBN-10: 1-56286-820-9
ISBN-13: 978-1-56286-820-8

ASTD Press Editorial Staff:
Director: Anthony Allen
Senior Manager, Production & Editorial: Glenn Saltzman
Community of Practice Manager, Human Capital: Kristin Husak
Associate Editor: Ashley McDonald
Associate Editor: Heidi Smith
Associate Editor: Stephanie Castellano
Design and Production: Abella Publishing Services, LLC
Cover Design: Ana Foreman

Printed by Versa Press, Inc., East Peoria, IL, www.versapress.com

10 STEPS TO SUCCESS

Let's face it, most people spend their days in chaotic, fast-paced, time- and resource-strained organizations. Finding time for just one more project, assignment, or even learning opportunity—no matter how career enhancing or useful—is difficult to imagine. The *10 Steps* series is designed for today's busy professional who needs advice and guidance on a wide array of topics ranging from project management to people management, from business strategy to decision making and time management, from leading effective meetings to researching and creating a compelling presentation. Each book in this ASTD series promises to take its readers on a journey to solid understanding, with practical application the ultimate destination. This is truly a just-tell-me-what-to-do-now series. You will find action-driven language teamed with examples, worksheets, case studies, and tools to help you quickly implement the right steps and chart a path to your own success. The *10 Steps* series will appeal to a broad business audience from middle managers to upper-level management. Workplace learning and human resource professionals, along with other professionals seeking to improve their value proposition in their organizations, will find these books a great resource.

C O N T E N T S

PREFACE

"Are your programs aligned with the organization? Are they connected to the business? Are you helping to meet our business goals? Is this project necessary? What's your contribution?" These and other similar questions from project sponsors bring into focus the issue of creating business alignment. A key issue in almost any type of project, alignment appears elusive, but can be routinely achieved and sustained for long periods of time. This book takes a fresh perspective on this challenging issue and shows how alignment is positioned early in the creation of projects, programs, and functions. It illustrates how to sustain alignment over a period of time and validate projects routinely to make sure that business alignment has been achieved.

The Need for This Book

Business analysts, professionals, managers, and executives need an uncomplicated reference to learn how to make alignment work. In 10 easy steps, this book shows how to align a program at the beginning, how to establish and support objectives to keep the focus on specific business measures throughout the life of the program, and how to validate that alignment has occurred as the influences from other factors are separated from the effects of the program.

You don't have to look far to find studies that reveal executive concern for business alignment. When the success or failure of projects or programs is explored, the results often boil down to the presence or lack of alignment. The authors recently conducted a study with *Fortune 500* CEOs regarding measures of success desired by executives. The executives suggested that business contribution, notably business impact, was their number-one desired measure. The study showed that 96 percent of the CEOs wanted to see impact data, although only 8 percent stated that they currently see this type of data. In a search for key words for this study, executives provided written comments about the need for business alignment, business contributions, and business connections.

In our own work at the ROI Institute, we have examined the reasons why projects fail. Each year, we have the opportunity to be involved in approximately 800 ROI studies, and many of them lack the success desired by the project owners. In short, some 30 to 40 percent of the studies are negative. Another 30 to 40 percent are positive, but still disappointing to the client. The remainder of the studies has more room for success. The number one reason for this lack of success is a failure to align the project to the business in the beginning. This is a critical issue.

Business alignment is necessary now more than ever. The global recession has intensified the need for business results from projects and functions in organizations. At the same time, there is mystery surrounding this process. How do you connect to the business for projects, programs, or functions? For example, the leadership development function has been challenged by some executives to show its value. Is it aligned to the business? Does it help drive key business measures, such as productivity? Is it possible for leadership development to show the value? Are new leadership development projects aligned to the business when implemented?

What This Book Will Do

Project or program managers don't always know how to connect the project to a business measure, let alone keep it focused on those measures throughout the project life cycle. While it is important to make the connection in the beginning, there is also a need to keep the focus on the business alignment through the project. At the same time, there is a need to verify that the alignment has occurred after the project is fully implemented. This is the validation that the project is indeed connected to the business and has improved one or more business measures. This particular issue, isolating the effects of the project, determines the precise contribution made by the project. This validation step is shrouded in even more mystery. This book attempts to unravel this alignment mystery in simple, rational terms, following a sequence of steps needed to generate a business connection that is CEO- and CFO-friendly.

Acknowledgments

We wish to acknowledge three groups of individuals who have helped us produce this book. The content of this book was developed with literally hundreds of clients over a period of two decades. We first published the alignment between needs assessment and evaluation in 1994 as a concept. Since then, we've refined this tool, currently labeled, the V-Model, which forms the basis for this book. Hundreds of clients have allowed us to work with them as we established the alignment of programs in the very beginning, kept the alignment through the process with impact objectives, and validated it on the follow-up.

We owe much appreciation to ASTD for their continued support of our work. This is our fortieth book with ASTD, our outstanding publishing partners. Our relationship with ASTD began with Nancy Olson's efforts in the 1990s and continuing to the present with Justin Brusino. For a publishing partnership to endure 40 titles is amazing in these turbulent times of short-term and strained partner relationships. We appreciate the patience and professionalism of ASTD in their quest to always be the leading provider of content in the field of human resource development.

Finally, much appreciation goes to Rachel Robinson for her excellent editing in this book. Rachel has taken on the challenge with short notice and has done an outstanding job of making this manuscript readable, enjoyable, and interesting to the audience. Thanks Rachel, for a great job. We look forward to many more publications.

Jack and Patti Phillips, 2012
jack@roiinstitute.net
patti@roiinstitute.net

INTRODUCTION

Business Alignment Issues

It is difficult to have a conversation about a project, program, event, initiative, or system without discussing the subject of business alignment. Some classic questions that are often asked about business projects are:

- How will this project help our business?
- Is this aligned to our goals?
- What is the business contribution?
- How is this helping my key performance indicators?
- What is the business value of this?
- How do we know this program has contributed to the business?
- Will the results of this project appear on my quarterly report?

These and similar questions focus on the issue of aligning projects and programs to the business. Programs must be aligned to the business early in their lives, throughout the implementation, and the business alignment must be validated after the program has been fully implemented and operational. Before we begin our discussion of the "10 steps" to business alignment, this introduction focuses on several key issues about business alignment and why it is presently a critical topic.

Definition

Business alignment is defined in a variety of ways. One definition from Business Dictionary is: the linking of organizational goals with the employees' personal goals.

The term business alignment is also used in regards to information technology, in which case it is defined by Wikipedia as: a desired state in which a business organization is able to use technology effectively to achieve business objectives—typically improved financial performance or marketplace competitiveness.

For this book we will define business alignment as: *ensuring that a new project, program, or process is connected directly to business impact measures, usually expressed in terms such as output, quality, cost, or time.* It is important for alignment to be verified in the beginning of the project; during the life of the project, there should be constant focus on the business measures to maintain the alignment. Steps are usually taken to validate the business alignment, confirming that the project contributed to improvements in one or more important business measures. While this definition is comprehensive, it clearly describes the focus of this book.

Types of Solutions That Need Business Alignment

Business alignment can be developed for almost every type of project. Inside the typical business organization, alignment will often be required or suggested in four major market areas: technology, quality, marketing, and human resources. In addition, projects in other support areas such as procurement, research and development, engineering, risk management, logistics, public relations, compliance, and legal should also focus on business alignment as projects

TABLE A

Projects Where Business Alignment Is Needed

Human Resources/Human Capital	Talent Retention Solutions
Training/Learning/Development	Project Management Solutions
Leadership/Coaching/Mentoring	Workforce Planning
Knowledge Management	Meetings/Events/Conferences
Organization Consulting/Development	Outsourcing Projects
Policies/Procedures/Processes	Communications/Public Relations
Recognition/Incentives/Engagement	Public Policy/Social Programs
Change Management	Risk Management/Ethics/Compliance
Technology/Systems/IT	Compensation and Benefits
Green Projects/Sustainability Projects	Wellness and Fitness Programs
Safety and Health Programs	Flexible Work Systems

are developed and implemented. The softer the process, the more mysterious the alignment issue, and this often leads to more requirements for business connection. For example, projects in human resources, public relations, and corporate communications are soft in nature and often spark an interest from top executives to ensure that new projects, programs, and various activities and functions in these areas are aligned to the business. Table A shows some typical programs and projects where alignment is a critical issue. This is only a starting point; alignment can occur in almost any area.

The Importance of Business Alignment

The issue of business alignment is reaching critical importance in organizations. When a project is properly aligned to the business, you and your organization will notice a huge difference. When it is not aligned, the results can be very disappointing and sometimes disastrous.

The Value of the Project

Sometimes the value of the project is reflected in the extent of the business alignment. Projects should be connected to the organization in terms of key business measures. When this is achieved, the value of the project is increased, particularly for those who fund and support it. Table B shows the new definition of value. An important part of this definition is the connection to business and sometimes the financial outcomes.

TABLE B
The "New" Definition of Value

Value must:
be linked to important business measures
be balanced, with qualitative and quantitative data
contain financial and non-financial perspectives
reflect strategic and tactical issues
satisfy all key stakeholders
be grounded in conservative standards
come from credible sources

Image of the Project

Projects that are not connected to business often suffer from an image perspective, while projects that are clearly connected have a more positive image. A business-aligned project earns executive respect and enhances the reputation of those who organize, control, implement, and even own these projects. This concept has evolved from the line versus staff distinction that permeated businesses decades ago. The line organization is the part of the business that produces and sells the project. In some cases the line focused on just those who produced the product. The other work was called staff, as they supported the line organization. The line was considered to be important, valuable, and essential, and often earned the full respect of the executive team. Staff, on the other hand, was often perceived as a necessary evil, not fully respected by the rest of the organization. From this concept, projects that are clearly aligned to important outcome measures such as output, quality, cost, and time have a very positive image, particularly if the measures are closely related to the principal mission of the organization.

Investing in the Project

Sometimes business alignment can determine whether or not a project is funded. Investment or funding decisions are usually made before a project is implemented. Also, investment decisions are made during a project to provide needed resources to keep the project going. After a project is completed, a decision is often made to invest in the same or similar projects in the future, based on the success of the project. In today's economy, lack of business alignment often results in lack of investment.

Supporting the Project

To be successful, projects must be supported by managers. Support is provided in a variety of ways, such as allocating resources for the projects, allowing people to be involved in them, giving time to make them successful, and verbally endorsing the projects. Managers and administrators will support projects when they view them as important, and aligning projects to the business increases the perceived importance of a project. If the projects are not aligned, importance—and thus support—will diminish quickly.

Project Approval

In some organizations, projects are only implemented if they are properly aligned to the business; otherwise they are not approved. By policy, procedure, or practice, some organizations will not approve the project unless there is a clear connection to the business, defined prior to the implementation of the project. Additionally, in these organizations, projects will not be continued unless the alignment is maintained. The alignment is a critical part of the projected success.

Collectively, these issues make alignment a critical topic that cannot be ignored, regardless of the particular function in the organization.

Who Needs Business Alignment?

The individuals who need business alignment are those who fund, support, and own the projects. To them, business alignment is essential, but there are many others who must be made aware of the connection to the business. Table C defines the stakeholders for typical projects and programs. While every one of these stakeholders can benefit from alignment, it is crucial to some more than others. The critical stakeholders are described in further detail below.

Figure A shows the interest in alignment with the different stakeholders, ranging from the highest level to the lowest level.

Drivers for Business Alignment

So what has happened to cause so much focus on business alignment these days? Hasn't it always been an issue? If not, what is causing it? Five major influences are driving this issue.

Trend toward Accountability

For the last two decades, there has been an obvious trend for more accountability in organizations. Executives have encouraged, supported, and even required others to be more accountable in driving important measures and outcomes. Figure B illustrates how different elements of a program's implementation have changed to focus

TABLE C

Stakeholders for Typical Projects and Programs

Stakeholder	Description
Stakeholder	Any individual or group interested in or involved in the program. Stakeholders may include the functional manager where the program is located, the participants, the organizer, the program leader, facilitators, and key clients, among others.
The Organization	The entity within which the particular project or program is evaluated. Organizations may be companies (either privately held or publicly held); government organizations at the local, state, federal, and international levels; nonprofits; or non-government organizations. They may also include educational institutions, associations, networks, and other loosely organized bodies of individuals.
Analyst	These individuals collect the data to determine whether the project is needed. They are also involved in analyzing various parts of the project. Analysts are usually more important in the beginning, but may provide helpful data throughout the project.
Bystanders	The individuals who observe the program, sometimes at a distance. They are not as actively involved as stakeholders, but are concerned about the outcomes, including the money. These bystanders are important, because they can become cheerleaders or critics of the project.
CEO/Managing Director/Agency Executive	The top executive in an organization. The top executive could be a plant manager, division manager, regional executive, administrator, or agency head. The CEO is the top administrator or executive in the operating entity where the project is implemented.
Evaluator	This person is responsible for measurement and evaluation, following all the processes outlined in this book. If this is a member of the project team, extreme measures must be taken to ensure this person remains objective. It may also be a person who is completely independent of the project. This individual performs these duties full- or part-time.

Table C, continued

Stakeholder	Description
Finance and Accounting Staff	These individuals are concerned about the cost and impact of the project from a financial perspective. They provide valuable support. Their approval of processes, assumptions, and methodologies is important. Sometimes, they are involved in the project evaluation; at other times they review the results. During major projects, this could include the organization finance director or chief financial officer.
Immediate Managers	The individuals who are one level above the participant(s) involved in the program or project. For some projects, this person is the team leader for other employees. Often they are middle managers, but most important, these people have supervisory authority over the participants in the project.
Participants	The individuals who are directly involved in the project. The term employee, associate, user, or stakeholder may represent these individuals. For most programs, the term participant appropriately reflects this group.
Project Designer/ Developer	The individuals who design and develop the project. The designers select and create the parameters for an effective and efficient project. The developers determine the content needed for success.
Project Manager	The individual(s) responsible for the project, program, initiative, or process. This is the individual who manages the project and is interested in showing the value of the project before it is implemented, during its implementation, and after it is implemented.
Project Team	The individuals involved in the project, helping to implement it. These are individual team members who may be full- or part-time on this particular project. On larger-scale projects, these individuals are often assigned full-time, on a temporary basis, or sometimes on a permanent basis. On small projects, these may be part-time duties.
Sponsor/Clients	The individual(s) who fund, initiate, request, or support a particular project or program. Sometimes referred to as the sponsor, it is the key group usually at the senior management level who cares about the project's success and is in a position to discontinue or expand the project.

FIGURE A

Interest in Business Alignment

Stakeholder	Interest Level
CEO/Top Administrator	High
Finance/Accounting Staff	
Sponsor/Client	↑
Immediate Managers of Participants	
Project Participants	
Project Team	Moderate
Project Evaluator	
Project Analysts	↑
Project Manager	
Bystander	
Project Designer/Developer	Low

on results, including the specific business measures. The previous approach, labeled activity management, focused on activities—sometimes ignoring what those activities were driving or delivering.

In the results-based approach, the process begins with the end in mind and exhibits clearly defined business measures. This requires alignment in the beginning of the process, at Step 1. The results-based approach has clearly shifted the thinking of stakeholders involved in projects.

Competition for Resources

Driven in part by the global competitive economy, organizations must be very mindful of their resources. Budgets are not unlimited, and there is always competition with others for those resources. Inside an organization, there is always another department, function, or unit needing more budget than has been approved. Sustaining alignment throughout the project is the best way to keep the resources flowing. Important, fully aligned projects get the most resources.

FIGURE B

Paradigm Shift in Programs

In Activity-Based Programs: ⟶	In Results-Based Programs:
• There is no business need for the program.	• The program is linked to specific business needs.
• There is no assessment of performance issues.	• There is an assessment of performance effectiveness.
• There are no specific measurable objectives.	• Specific objectives are set for application and business impact.
• There is no effort to prepare program participants to achieve results.	• The results expectations are communicated to participants.
• There is no effort to prepare the work environment to support the program.	• The environment is prepared to support the program.
• There are no efforts to build partnerships with key managers.	• Partnerships are established with key managers and clients.
• There is no measurement of results or cost benefit analysis.	• There is a measurement of results or cost benefit analysis (ROI).
• The reporting on programs is input focused.	• Reporting on programs is output focused.

Lean/Mean/Efficient Mentality

Organizations have experienced many change processes starting with a total quality management and moving through re-engineering, transformation, Six Sigma, lean engineering, lean Six Sigma, and various other processes. These processes have much in common in terms of attempting to make the organization more efficient and effective. By increasing efficiency, these processes focus directly on business measures and ensure that projects, programs, and activities are clearly connected to those measures.

Global Recessions

The most recent global recession, coupled with others that have occurred and probably those that will continue to evolve, focused additional efforts on business alignment. The 2008-2011 global recession produced a mandate from executives to ensure that every new project or program is clearly connected to the business. Each program must add value and in many cases, must add value that exceeds the cost of the project. These recessions have a way of stimulating the efficient use of processes that often stay with the organization after the recession is over.

Top Executive Requirements

Finally, top executives are demanding alignment. They will no longer accept investing in projects on faith. They want to see evidence, even proof. Even for the hard functions of quality and technology, executives want to see a clear line of sight to the business in a very credible way. They have adopted a theme of, "show me the money." Figure C shows how this has evolved from "show me some data" to "show me the ROI."

FIGURE C

Executive Focus on Projects and Programs

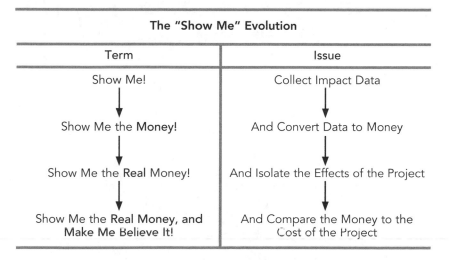

The "Show Me" Evolution

Term	Issue
Show Me!	Collect Impact Data
↓	↓
Show Me the **Money!**	And Convert Data to Money
↓	↓
Show Me the **Real** Money!	And Isolate the Effects of the Project
↓	↓
Show Me the **Real Money, and Make Me Believe It!**	And Compare the Money to the Cost of the Project

Collectively, these five drivers make business alignment a critical necessity, not something simply to be done when it is convenient.

The V-Model: The Tool of Business Alignment

The V-model is the tool with which business alignment becomes a visible process. Figure D shows the connection between evaluation and needs assessment for projects and programs. This figure shows the important linkage between the initial problem or opportunity that created the need for the program, and the evaluation of the

FIGURE D

Business Alignment with the V-Model

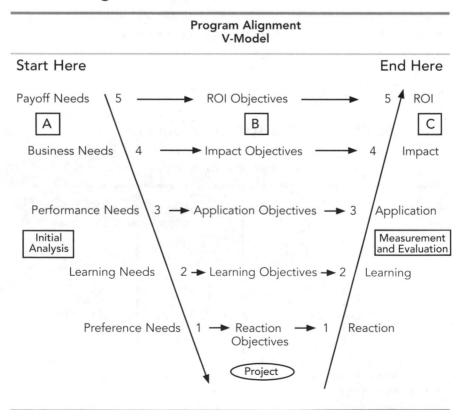

program. It also shows the three points at which business alignment occurs: at the beginning of the project (A), during the project (B), and during the follow up evaluation (C), in order to validate the alignment.

The V-Model is based on the concept of levels which has been used for centuries to express increased value at a higher level. For example, when something is said to be moved to "the next level," it is suggested that the new level is more valuable than its predecessor. It's best to think of the V-Model in terms of the evaluation side first. Evaluation of a particular project or program moves through different levels of measuring:

◆ Reaction to the program (Level 1).
◆ Learning skills and knowledge to make the program successful (Level 2).
◆ Application of skills and knowledge in the workplace (Level 3).
◆ Impact measures linked to the program (Level 4).
◆ ROI, a comparison of monetary benefits to the cost of the program (Level 5).

From the viewpoint of a program's key stakeholders, such as the clients or sponsors, moving evaluation to the next level represents increased value, as most clients want to see the business contribution (Level 4) and even sometimes ROI (Level 5). In terms of evaluation of the program, it is at Level 4 that the effect of the program will be isolated on the data to indicate specifically how much improvement is connected to this particular program. When this is accomplished, the business alignment for the program is validated.

The measures that are captured at each level are defined in the objectives. There are five corresponding levels of objectives, as illustrated in Figure D. The business impact objective is the alignment through the program. When there is an impact objective, all the stakeholders are focused on the ultimate goal of the program in terms of business contribution. The focus is there for the organizers, designers, developers, facilitators, participants, managers of participants, and others who have interest in the program. The objectives increase in value as the levels progress, with levels four and five being the most valuable from a client's perspective. These objectives are developed during the needs assessment. The needs assessment defines particular needs at each level. Here, the highest and most important level is the potential payoff of the program, followed by business needs, performance needs, learning needs, and preference needs.

How the V-Model Works

At Level 5, the potential payoff needs for the program are addressed. This step examines the possibility for a return on investment before the program is pursued. At Level 4, the business needs that precipitated the need for consulting are examined. At Level 3, the specific performance that must change or action that must be taken to meet the business needs is defined. At Level 2, the specific information, knowledge, or skills that are required to address the performance needs are identified. This is a classic learning needs assessment. Finally, the preferences for the program define the Level 1 needs. This connection is very important for understanding all of the elements that make up a successful program or project.

Using the V-Model

The V-Model provides a very effective way to examine any project or program. It clearly shows the points of alignment and it shows the client and sponsor how the entire project framework is developed. It represents an extremely useful way to illustrate the connection between the up-front analysis and evaluation of the follow up. The objectives provide the transition between the two. The appendix of the book contains several examples of V-Models to show how they can be implemented for a variety of projects and programs.

Payoff Needs

The first part of the process is to determine if the problem is worth solving or the opportunity warrants serious consideration. In some cases, this is obvious when there are serious problems that are affecting the organization's operations and strategy. For example, at a hospital, an annual turnover of critical talent at 35 percent is an obvious payoff opportunity, and thus has potential payoff written all over it. In another example, new account growth is flat and customer loyalty is low, based on industry standards. These types of payoff opportunities make it clear that this is a problem that needs to be solved or an opportunity that should be pursued with a clearly identified business need.

Some requests represent not-so-obvious payoff opportunities such as a request to implement leadership competencies for all middle level managers or establish a project management office. It is not clear what business measures will actually change as a result of these projects. The focus at the next level (Level 4) is to clearly define the business measure or measures. In an experimental project of converting employees to a work-at-home arrangement, the initial request to reduce employee travel time in order to lower costs and have a positive impact on the environment was not so obvious in terms of payoff. A work-at-home solution was anticipated. Additional detail was needed, and this need led to the connection of several measures. These requests may be difficult for the not-so-obvious opportunities and may raise concerns. The project may not be connected to business needs, and if it isn't, the client should be made aware.

At this level, it is important not only to identify the business measures that need to improve, but also to convert them into monetary values so the anticipated improvement can be converted to money. The "show me the money" requirement is occurring more often these days. The second part of the process is to develop an approximate cost for the entire project. This could come from a detailed proposal or even a rough estimate. At this stage, only an estimate is necessary. The projected cost of the project is then compared to the potential monetary benefits to show the ROI forecast. A forecast of ROI is important in very expensive, strategic, or critical projects. This step may be omitted in a situation when the problem must be solved regardless of the cost. For example, as an organization strives to be a socially responsible leader, it may be difficult to place a monetary value on the goal.

Business Needs: The First Point of Alignment

At Level 4, business data are examined to determine which measures need to improve. This involves a review of organizational records and reports, examining all types of hard and soft data. It is usually the performance of one of the data items that triggers the consulting project. For example, when market share is not as much as it should be, operating costs are excessive, product quality is deteriorating, or productivity is low, the business measure is easily pinpointed. These are key issues that come directly from the data in the organization and are often found in the operating reports or records.

Business needs are sometimes arranged in categories of hard data to include output, quality, cost, and time. Examples are sales, production, errors, waste, accidents, costs, downtime, project time, and compliance fines. These measures exist in any type of organization, even in the public sector and among nonprofits and nongovernment organizations (NGOs). These measures often attract the attention of executives, as they represent business impact. An important goal is to connect the project to one or more of these issues.

Sometimes impact measures are more on the soft side, which includes customer service, image, work climate, customer satisfaction, job satisfaction, engagement, reputation, and teamwork. Although these may not be perceived to be as important as hard data, they are still important, and in many cases, a project will be connected to several soft data items. This book defines a soft measure that can be converted to money as "tangible." If it cannot be converted to money credibly, with a minimum amount of resources, it is left as an "intangible." This definition suggests that most of the hard data categories are usually converted to money and are thus tangible.

Performance Needs

The Level 3 analysis involves determining performance needs. The task is to determine what is causing the problem (or creating the opportunity) identified at Level 4 (e.g. what is causing the business to be below the desired level). Something in the system is not performing as it should and may include, among other things, the following:

◆ inappropriate behavior
◆ dysfunctional behavior
◆ ineffective systems
◆ improper process flow
◆ ineffective procedures
◆ unsupported processes
◆ inappropriate technology
◆ inaction of stakeholders.

The analysis usually reveals that a group of people are not performing as they should. The reason for this inadequate performance is the basis for the solution, the project. For example, if employee health care costs are increasing more than they should and sick leave usage is increasing, the cause may be unhealthy habits of employees. A wellness and fitness program may be needed.

Performance needs must be uncovered using a variety of problem-solving or analysis techniques. This may involve the use of data collection techniques discussed in this book, such as surveys, questionnaires, focus groups, or interviews. It may involve a variety of problem-solving or analytical techniques such as root-cause analysis, fish-bone diagrams, and other analysis techniques. Whatever is used, the key is to determine all of the causes of the problem so that solutions can be developed. Often, multiple solutions are appropriate.

Learning Needs

The analysis at Level 2 usually uncovers specific learning needs for the participants involved in the project. The analysis may reveal learning deficiencies, in terms of knowledge and skills, that can contribute to the problem if they are not the major cause of it. In other situations, the solution will need a learning component as participants learn how to implement a new process, procedure, or technology. The learning typically involves acquisition of knowledge or the development of skills necessary to improve performance. In some cases, perceptions or attitudes may need to be altered to make the process successful in the future. The extent of learning required will determine whether formalized training is needed or if more informal, on-the-job methods can be utilized to build the necessary skills and knowledge.

Preference Needs

The final level is to consider the preference for the project solution. This involves determining the preferred way in which those involved in the process will need or want it to be implemented. A fundamental issue at this level is the perceived value of the project. Typical questions that surface are, "Is this important?" "Is this necessary?" and "Is it relevant to me?" Preference needs may involve implementation issues, including decisions such as when learning is expected and in what amounts, how it is presented, and the overall time frame. Implementation issues may involve timing, support, expectations, and other key factors. The important issue is to try to determine the specific preferences to the greatest extent possible so that the complete profile of the solution can be developed based on all of the needs.

Objectives

It is easy to see that the detailed needs analysis at the different levels yields the objectives for the particular project or program. Ideally, for projects involving major resources and those of significant importance to the organization, a thorough needs assessment should be conducted and corresponding objectives should be developed at all levels. Perhaps the ROI objective can be omitted, but having impact and application objectives is very critical. The application objectives detail what individuals should be doing to make the project successful. In terms of formal learning and development, this is typically the use of the skills. Impact objectives are the consequence of those skills and represent the business measure that was identified in the original business needs analysis. This provides a focus on business during the project, ensuring that alignment is a top priority for all of those involved, particularly the participants and the facilitators in a formal learning setting. Objectives are developed to be very specific, often with accuracy, quality, and time specifications. More detail on objectives is provided in Step 6.

Levels of Evaluation

The levels of evaluation, as previously described, provide the framework for data collection to measure the success of the project. The levels of evaluation build on the objectives. Objectives define precisely what is measured, and often include the definition of success for that measure. These are classic levels for all types of projects and programs. These levels date back to John Quincy Adams, as he developed levels of effectiveness of leaders. Adams suggested that leaders cause others to dream more (Level 1), learn more (Level 2), do more (Level 3), and become more (Level 4). Additional information on levels of evaluation can be found in later chapters.

What Happens When Alignment Is Not Achieved?

When business alignment is not achieved the potential advantages of a project, program, or function are not seen, and the opposite of the desired effects often develops. Below is a summary of some straightforward consequences that can result.

◆ Funding will suffer when business alignment is not evident.

◆ Support is necessary for success; if a project is not connected to something meaningful in the organization, its importance and support will diminish.

◆ A variety of support functions are seeking influence, such as technology, marketing, human resources, risk management, and others. When these functions are aligned to the business, they will gain influence; and without such alignment, influence could dwindle or disappear completely.

◆ Proper business alignment builds relationships with key business partners who will support you, request your services, and help reward you in many ways. Without it, the relationship deteriorates.

◆ The image of functions often suffers without connection to the business. This is particularly true for the soft processes of communications, public relations, government affairs, leadership development, and change management; these areas must strive for business alignment in order to be supported and sustained.

Final Thoughts

Business alignment is critical and essential. This introduction outlines why it should be undertaken and where to begin. The V-Model clearly shows what steps must be taken to ensure alignment is achieved at the beginning of the project, as it is connected to business need. It also ensures that appropriate impact objectives are developed to keep the project focused and connected to a business measure throughout its implementation. Finally, on the follow-up, when post-program data are collected, the business measure is monitored as part of the evaluation at Level 4, impact evaluation. When the impact of the program is isolated on the business data, the resulting business contribution is clearly defined, showing the proof that the program or project made a difference. The V-Model is an extremely helpful tool in ensuring business alignment is achieved and maintained. There are many reasons why alignment occurs and there are many advantages for having alignment. As a process, business alignment can no longer be ignored.

Discuss Business Alignment with Clients

Not all projects are appropriate for business alignment.

Communication with the client should be clear and open.

There are five critical areas of discussion.

The best time to have the initial discussion with the client about the business alignment issue is at the conception of the project. The preparation necessary for these conversations is a full understanding about the value of business alignment and the key issues involved in the V-model, the alignment process (covered in the Introduction). This chapter, the first step to business alignment, explores the necessary conversations that must be conducted early, not only to explain the concept of business alignment to the client, but also to move the project to the desired alignment. This is important, particularly when the requested or planned project is not so clearly connected to the business.

Discussing business alignment with a client may require a bit of explaining, informing, persuading, encouraging, and recommending as particular steps, issues, thoughts, or cautions are explored. These conversations may occur in an environment where a client is not interested in having additional dialogue. Sometimes the client is resistant to any discussion that changes the project in any way after the initial request. These types of discussions can be sensitive and thus must be subtle, diplomatic, and persuasive, and at the same time, not forceful or demanding. Five key issues are addressed in this first step.

Should This Project Be Aligned to the Business?

Not every project should be aligned to the business. At the same time, some should always be aligned to the business, and there are many in between. The first issue is to sort out which projects are appropriate for business alignment, and to discuss this issue with the client. Table 1.1 outlines the selection criteria for programs that are ideal for business alignment, those that may be more appropriate to be aligned to application instead of business, and those that may not need to be aligned to the business.

Impact and ROI

In the first category for selecting projects for business alignment is the life cycle of the proposed project. Sometimes a project will have a long life cycle once it is fully implemented. When this is the case, perhaps the project should be aligned to the business to make sure that the business value is there. Conversely, if the project is short term, such as a one shot effort, it may not be necessary to align it to the business.

The most critical projects for alignment are the ones that are tied directly to goals or operational issues. Almost by design, these projects are usually connected to the business, but they may lack the specificity and detailed connection to business measures. Obviously, these are great candidates for business alignment.

The extent that a project supports strategic objectives is important. Sometimes a project is initiated because of a particular strategic objective. When this is the case, business alignment is absolutely essential. In other cases top executives are interested in the alignment because of the strategic linkage or perceived linkage

TABLE 1.1

Which Projects Are Ideal for Business Alignment?

Criteria for Selecting Projects for Business Alignment

- Life cycle of the project
- Linkage of project to operational goals and issues
- Importance of project to strategic objectives
- Top executives' interest in the alignment
- Cost of the project
- Visibility of the project
- Size of the target audience
- Investment of time in the project

Criteria for Selecting Projects for Application Alignment

- Short cycle projects
- Projects where application is critical
- Projects where behavior change is critical
- Compliance projects
- Skill-based projects

Projects That Are Not Necessarily Ideal for Business Alignment

- Entry level projects
- Job related skills
- Very brief projects
- Very inexpensive projects

to strategy. In these cases, senior executives are requiring evidence of a project's alignment to the business. The logic is straightforward: If it is important enough to drive strategy, it is important enough to be measured at the impact and ROI levels.

The cost of the particular project often forces business alignment. Expensive projects must be connected to the business, while inexpensive projects may not necessarily require a connection. The visibility of the project is sometimes an issue. Highly visible projects often bring out the critics and they will ask for accountability, including the business connection. Sometimes the size of the target audience is important. If the project involves 20,000 employees when it is fully implemented and each person will have to take time to be involved in the activities or processes, then it becomes important enough to connect it to the business.

If a project involves only 10 people in the legal department, alignment to the business may not be necessary. Finally, when large amounts of time and resources are committed to a project, the project should be connected to the business in most cases.

Collectively, these important issues drive the need to connect to business measures. These criteria should be considered together for the selection of ROI projects, or in a system to make sure each criterion is given the proper weight.

Application

Sometimes projects should stop with alignment at the application level. This requires that the project be clearly defined at the very beginning, classifying what new actions, processes, or behavior must be in place for the project to be successful. Objectives should be set at the application level and the follow-up data should show that the application has occurred. Certain projects can stop the alignment at this level, which is short of the business alignment level. These are often projects that are very short cycle, maybe one-time projects that potentially have an urgent need to be completed. Sometimes projects require specific behavior or process steps. For example, in a software implementation project, the technology is already in place but some individuals may need to be prepared to use the software appropriately. Application alignment is probably most important. Sometimes behavior is the most important issue, particularly with soft programs that involve topics such as communications, public relations, leadership development, and organizational change. Again, application is probably most important.

Many new compliance programs are based on application. In order to be in compliance, employees must be operating in a particular way (application). When compliance is based solely on application, perhaps the alignment is needed only at that level. When projects are based on acquiring necessary information for a particular job, it may not be necessary for the project to advance to business level, but end at the application level.

When Is a Project Not Appropriate for Business Alignment?

Finally, some programs are not appropriate for business alignment. Projects where compliance is defined at Level 2 or even 0 are not good candidates for business alignment. For example, some compliance projects mean that every individual must have exposure to a particular topic or issue. This exposure is defined as input in the project and it is often referred to as Level 0. Sometimes compliance is defined by individuals only having awareness of a certain issue. When this is the case, the compliance is based on learning, which is Level 2.

Technical requirements for jobs are absolutely essential for the work to be done. Projects involving job-needed skills or requirements are not good candidates for business alignment. Projects involving new employees are often improbable candidates for business alignment because the project involves necessary job requirements, so business alignment may not be necessary. Very brief programs and projects do not make practical candidates either. For example, a one hour e-learning project to show a sales team how to cross-sell a particular product may not need business alignment as it is both very inexpensive and short.

In summary, as Table 1.1 illustrates, there are some very general guidelines to help to select programs for business alignment. These are only suggestions. Beyond those criteria, there may be other indicators that suggest when project alignment is needed at the business level.

Clarifying Business Alignment Expectations

Although the client may know about the concept of business align-ment and may even request it, sometimes they are unsure of what it actually means and how it is developed. The process covered in this book is comprehensive and remarkably user friendly. It is also a process that is used by thousands of organizations to achieve business alignment. Part of the process of communicating with the client is to clearly understand their expectations, addressing the is-sues in Table 1.2.

Balanced Set of Data

The first issue is to define the different types of data. The V-Model alignment in this book offers up to five levels of data. The client should understand that all these data sets are captured in the busi-ness alignment process. When alignment is made at the business level (Level 4), alignment is also necessary at Levels 3, 2, and 1. As an optional part of the business alignment, ROI can be developed. The decision may be made in the beginning of the project to en-sure that the ROI is a part of the alignment. For some, the ROI, or the monetary value of the business improvement compared to the cost of the program, represents the ultimate business alignment. When calculating the actual ROI, some measures cannot be convert-ed to money credibly with a reasonable amount of resources. These are the intangibles and they are very important alignment data. Clients are usually pleased with the different data sets that can be aligned to the project.

Credibility of the Process

It is important for the client to understand that the methodology being used in this book is credible and builds on the success of over 4,000 organizations in 58 countries. It uses consistent catego-ries of data collected in a step-by-step process. Conservative stan-dards are involved in the analysis. Throughout use of the

TABLE 1.2

The Case for Business Alignment

Balanced Data Set

1. Reaction and Planned Action	Measures participant reaction to the project and captures planned actions, if appropriate.
2. Learning	Measures changes in knowledge, skills, and attitudes related to the project.
3. Application and Implementation	Measures changes in on-the-job behavior or actions as the project is applied, implemented, or utilized.
4. Business Impact	Measures changes in business impact variables (tangible and intangible).
5. Return on Investment	Compare project monetary benefits to the costs.

Business Alignment Follows a Very Credible Methodology

- Common categories of data
- Systematic, step-by-step process
- Conservative standards
- Results-based approach
- High level of use
- Client focused
- Satisfies all stakeholders

Business Alignment Provides a Payoff

- Show contributions of selected projects.
- Justify/defend project funding.
- Identify inefficient projects that need to be redesigned or eliminated.
- Improve image of function.
- Earn a "seat at the table."

- Align project to business needs.
- Earn respect of senior management/administrators.
- Improve support for project.
- Enhance design and implementation processes.
- Identify successful projects that can be implemented in other areas.

entire process, there is a focus on results. With the extensive applications, it is estimated that at least 5,000 projects a year achieve business alignment using this methodology. The process is very client focused as it requires routine communication and input from clients. Finally, it satisfies the different stakeholders involved, particularly at the C-suite level, including CEO and CFO.

The Payoff

Another important conversation to have with clients is the payoff of the alignment process. As Table 1.2 shows, there are many reasons for achieving business alignment. Most clients clearly understand the issue of funding. Adequate funding must be provided and maintained throughout the project. Business alignment is one of the best ways to justify and defend business projects. It helps to drive process improvement and program redesign when things are not working so well. Proper business alignment will also build respect for the function where the project is located, improve support of the project, and help to build relationships with executives. The key issue is to brief the client about the importance of business alignment and the expected outcome of achieving alignment with business measures.

Review the Current Status

The current status of alignment is reviewed by using the V-Model. When using the V-Model, the client discussion should focus on the current status of the project and its movement toward business impact. The approach for this is detailed in Table 1.3 and begins with the issue of the proper time to bring up the alignment. Following the discussion in the previous section, alignment should always be kept at the forefront of client conversations. Business alignment should always be mentioned as a possibility. The concept should be fully explained and explored when there is interest. Sometimes it should be pushed or required when it becomes obvious that the project should be aligned to the business.

TABLE 1.3

The Message to Clients

When to Mention Alignment

- Always mention the results-based approach.
- Mention business alignment as a possibility.
- Explain business alignment—when there is interest.
- Push business alignment—when it should be considered.
- Require alignment—when it is a must.

Business Alignment Details

- Because of the critical importance of this project, alignment is built into the project.
- Data collection, analysis, and reporting will be handled by an external group.
- Your involvement will be necessary, but minimal.
- You will receive a detailed impact study, and executive summary, and a one-page summary.
- The study will contain recommendations for improving the project (process improvement).
- The results will be presented to key stakeholders.

Additional Questions

- What are the objectives for the project at each level?
- Is this a problem worth solving?
- Is there a potential payoff?
- What is the specific business measure?
- What happens if we do nothing?
- What is occurring or not occurring on the job that influences the business measure?
- What skills or knowledge is needed to support the job performance need?
- How should the solution be structured?

Business Alignment Is Feasible

- It's not very expensive.
- Many shortcut methods are available.
- Time requirements can be easily managed.
- It fits all types of projects.
- Technology helps with costs/time.
- Implementation is planned/systematic.

Business Alignment Details and Questions

It is important to discuss the details involved and show what steps are necessary to achieve proper business alignment for projects. Clients must also be aware of what they will receive in exchange for their extra efforts as they approach the alignment process and become involved with it. Additional questions direct the attention to the business measure. These questions are essential to ensure that the alignment is achieved when it is not so obvious that the project is connected to the business. Additional questions and probing issues are covered in subsequent chapters. Sometimes there are obvious alignment opportunities when the project is presented with business measures clearly defined. In other situations, the business measure is not as clearly defined and it must be developed. In between those two extremes there is often confusion, and these types of questions will help direct the client to the proper business measure.

Business Alignment Feasibility

The client must understand that alignment is feasible and can be achieved within resources needed for the project. Rarely does the alignment piece cost additional money. If the alignment does lead to further costs, it should only involve a few questions in the beginning and then during the follow-up. If the follow-up is planned the only additional step is to isolate the effects of the programs on the business data. If follow-up is not planned, that piece will have to be added to ensure that alignment was achieved in the process.

Success Factors for Achieving Alignment

Most clients want to know what can make the project successful, particularly as it is aligned to the business and as the business connection is tracked throughout the process. Table 1.4 defines those success factors.

TABLE 1.4

Success Factors for Business Alignment

Set the Ground Rules

- Business alignment is a process improvement tool designed to improve projects.
- Business alignment is not designed for performance review for individuals.
- Every project reveals opportunities for changes.
- Negative results represent the best opportunity to learn.
- Negative results have a positive story.
- Don't wait for a client to ask for business alignment.

Before the Project Is Initiated

- Clients commit to business alignment.
- Alignment with business measures is achieved.
- Specific objectives for application and impact are developed.
- Performance issues are addressed.
- Participants commit to drive results and provide data.
- Content is focused on application and impact.

During the Project

- Impact objectives are in place.
- Projects are facilitated with application/impact in mind.
- Effective data collection methods are used.
- Specific strategies are implemented to transfer learning to the job.
- Participants provide adequate data.

After the Project Is Completed

- Alignment is validated (results isolated to the project).
- Business alignment follows conservative standards.
- Results are communicated to key stakeholders.
- Results are used to drive improvement.
- Results are used to market/fund future projects.

The Ground Rules

The process begins with the ground rules. It is important that the client fully understands what must happen in order for the project to be successful. First, the client or sponsor must clearly understand that this is a process improvement tool designed to improve projects and programs. This process is not necessary for performance review of participants or owners. Usually the project fails because of other influences. This could be a debatable issue, but projects are usually not successful when the failure of the project is considered part of the performance review for those people involved in it.

For some projects, the project managers must be held accountable, and this is an appropriate understanding when defined beforehand. Participants are attracted to a project's impact and success as it is linked to business measures. However, not many individuals want to be involved in a project as participants if their performance evaluation is affected by influences outside of their control. The primary reason for the project failing is not always the project itself or the participants and the stakeholders who are charged with making it work. Failure comes from other influences and perhaps even lack of support from the managers of participants.

An important ground rule is to pursue business alignment on a proactive basis and not wait on the request from top executives. Unfortunately, this is not always the approach. Too many program organizers wait until executives force the issue. This places the team on the executives' agenda, often with a short time frame to show business results.

Program Implementation

Before the project is initiated, several factors must be considered as shown in Table 1.5. This list provides the client with an understanding of what the different stakeholders must do to make the project successful. Most of these are addressed during alignment discussions. During the project, the impact objectives drive the alignment through the process. The success factors focus on the role of participants, facilitators, and data collection. Finally, after the project is completed, the alignment is validated with the extra step to isolate the effects of the project on the data. A few more issues are necessary for that alignment to be completed and validated. Collectively these issues can make the difference in success or failure of a project from a business alignment perspective.

Resources and Roles to Achieve Success

The final question often raised by clients is: "What is my role and what are the roles of others to make this project successful as it is aligned to the business?" Essentially, the requirement of business alignment makes a project a little different for some, because previously these types of projects may not have been connected to the business. Extra effort is needed throughout the project and during the follow up. Aligning a project to the business also requires a different mindset for all individuals involved who must accept responsibility and be open to accountability of driving business success with this project. Table 1.5 shows the various roles of the stakeholders involved in the project. This provides a quick checklist for ensuring that everyone is aware of what is necessary to achieve success.

It is important for the individual who is selling the alignment to the client to build rapport. This may be the project owner, project developer, or other stakeholder. This individual ensures that the alignment is achieved in the beginning and that the objectives are developed to align the project throughout its implementation. This individual will also ensure that the alignment is validated for the follow-up.

Within Table 1.5 is a list of the client roles and a brief description of what is required of each. This is similar to the success factors detailed earlier but now provides clear specifics of what must be achieved. The analyst's role ensures that the project is aligned

TABLE 1.5

Roles in Business Alignment Projects

Projects Owner's Role in Business Alignment (the person selling alignment)

- Understand business alignment.
- Explain business alignment.
- Encourage business alignment.
- Use business alignment data properly.
- Use business alignment results in strategic marketing.

Client's Role in Business Alignment

- Understand business alignment.
- Support business alignment.
- Provide resources for business alignment studies.
- Use business alignment data properly.
- Embrace business alignment as process improvement.

Analyst's Role in Business Alignment

- Ensure the program/project is needed.
- Connect program to business need.
- Develop objectives at multiple levels.

Designer's/Developer's Role in Business Alignment

- Clarify objectives.
- Relate content to application/impact.
- Include application/impact in exercises/activities.

Participant's Role in Business Alignment

- Be involved in project.
- Learn the content.
- Apply the content.
- Achieve results (impact).
- Provide data when needed.

at the beginning, often under the direction of the project owner. The designer/developer will ensure that the content of the project clearly connects to the business, using exercises, simulations, skill practices, tools, and other processes that make up the content of the project.

Table 1.5, continued

Facilitator's/Coordinator's Role in Business Alignment
• Begin with the end in mind.
• Teach to application/impact objectives.
• Require action plans and other application tools.
• Be involved in follow-up.

Evaluation Team's Role in Business Alignment
• Complete evaluation planning.
• Design data collection instruments.
• Collect data.
• Analyze data.
• Report results.
• Drive improvement.

The participants' roles must also be clearly defined. These are the individuals who will ultimately make the project successful. They are always expected to be involved and fully engaged in the project, and to ensure that various project activities are completed. This has expanded now to include securing the business results. Otherwise the project will not be successful. Also, these participants often have to provide data that is necessary to show the value of the project, particularly for the impact measures on the follow-up evaluation.

The roles of the facilitators and coordinators are relatively straightforward, although their involvement may be higher than usual. The facilitator is now responsible for driving impact objectives, which indicate they must take the project through to the changes in business measures. For some, this may be uncomfortable, particularly for a project that has a longer time period for achievement. They prefer to be held accountable to the activities that are inherent at the application level. Also, for learning and development programs, facilitators quickly suggest that they have no influence on the success of the project beyond the classroom and are merely coordinating some of the activities. However, having impact objectives clearly detailed ensures that they properly influence the achievement of business improvement.

Finally the role of the evaluation team is very straightforward. With business objectives in hand, it is easy to plan the evaluation, collect and analyze the data, and report the results. Without clear objectives all the way through to business impact, this task is difficult. With proper objectives in place, evaluation becomes much easier.

Final Thoughts

Communicating with a client is the first of 10 steps for achieving business alignment. This is a step that if not done properly will jeopardize the entire process. The client must fully understand what is involved and what is needed to achieve business alignment for the project. Pushing the project to business alignment often elevates it to a higher level of accountability. While this brings on a bit of extra work, it can also bring additional exposure that must be managed throughout the process.

The client has a critical role in the success of the project, the actual alignment, and of influencing others to step up to this level of accountability. This step fully explored the five critical areas for this additional discussion. The next step focuses on determining the payoff needs.

Determine Payoff Needs

OVERVIEW

Needs must be defined early in order to set proper objectives.

All payoff opportunities should be examined, even when they are not so obvious.

Examine *all* costs and their implications.

If needs are not defined clearly and early in the process, a flawed project or program can result, creating inefficiencies and other problems. This chapter explores payoff needs, the second step for business alignment. The image of the V-model presented in the Introduction (Figure D) will prove helpful as analysis begins. In the next four steps we will assess the needs at five levels, beginning with payoff needs and progressing to preference needs. The objectives derived directly from these needs are defined, making a case for multiple levels of objectives that correspond with specific needs. The objectives serve as the transition from needs assessment to evaluation.

The Importance of Payoff

The highest level of alignment, return-on-investment, comes from an analysis of payoff needs. This initial step begins with a few crucial questions:

- Is this program worth doing?
- Does this address an issue worth pursuing?

- Is this an opportunity?
- Is it a feasible program?
- What is the likelihood of a positive ROI?

The answers to these questions are obvious for proposed projects or programs that address significant problems or opportunities with potentially high rewards. The questions might take longer to answer for lower-profile programs or those for which the possible payoff is less apparent. In any case, these are legitimate questions, and the analysis can be simple or comprehensive. Figure 2.1 shows the potential payoff in monetary terms. A program's payoff comes in the form of either profit increases or in cost savings (derived from cost reduction or cost avoidance).

Profit increases are generated by programs that improve sales, increase market share, introduce new products, open new markets, enhance customer service, or increase customer loyalty. These should pay off with increases in sales revenue. Other revenue-generating measures include increasing memberships, increasing donations, obtaining grants, and generating tuition from new and returning students—all of which, after taking out the cost of doing business, yield a profit.

FIGURE 2.1

The Payoff Opportunity

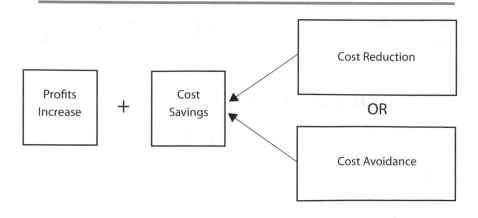

However, most programs pay off with cost savings generated through cost reduction or cost avoidance. For example, learning and development programs that improve quality, reduce cycle time, lower downtime, decrease complaints, prevent employee turnover, and minimize delays are all examples of cost savings. When the goal is solving a problem, monetary value is often based on cost reduction.

Cost-avoidance programs aim to reduce risks, avoid problems, or prevent unwanted events. Some may view cost avoidance as an inappropriate measure for developing monetary benefits and calculating ROI. However, if the assumptions are correct, an avoided cost (for example, compliance fines) can yield a higher reward than an actual cost reduction. Preventing a problem is more cost-effective than waiting for it to occur and then having to resolve it.

Determining potential payoff is the first step in the needs analysis process. Closely related is the next step, determining business need, as the potential payoff is often based on improvements or changes in business measures. Determining the payoff involves two factors: 1) the potential monetary value derived from the business measure's improvement and 2) the approximate cost of the program or project. Developing these monetary values in detail usually yields a more credible forecast of the defined solution. However, this step may be omitted in situations where the business need must be resolved regardless of the program cost, or when resolution of the business need has an obviously a high payoff. For example, if the problem involves a safety concern, a regulatory compliance issue, or a very critical issue, then a detailed analysis of the payoff is unnecessary.

Identifying the Need

A needs analysis should begin with several questions. Table 2.1 presents some questions to ask about a proposed program. The answers to these questions might make the case for proceeding without analysis or they may indicate the need for additional analysis.

TABLE 2.1

Key Questions to Ask About the Proposed Program

STEP 2

• Why is this an issue?	• Are there multiple solutions?
• Who will support the program?	• What happens if we do nothing?
• Who will not support the program?	• How much will the solution(s) cost?
• Are there important intangible benefits?	• Is a forecast needed?
• How can we fund the program?	• Is there a potential payoff (positive ROI)?
• Is this issue critical?	• Is this issue linked to strategy?
• Is it possible to correct it?	• Is it feasible to improve it?
• How much is it costing us?	• Can we find a solution?

The answers could show that the program is not needed. Understanding the implications of moving forward (or not) can reveal the legitimacy of the proposed program.

The good news is, for many potential programs, answers to these questions are readily available. The need may have already been realized and the consequences validated. For example, many organizations with an employee-retention problem within a critical talent group have calculated the cost of employee turnover. This cost is either developed from existing data or secured from similar studies. With this cost in hand, the economic impact of the problem is known. The proposed program's cost can be compared to the problem's cost (in this case, excessive turnover) to get a sense of potential added value. The cost of the program can usually be estimated if a solution has been tentatively identified.

Obvious Payoff Opportunities

The potential payoff is obvious for some programs, but not so obvious for others. Table 2.2 lists some opportunities with obvious payoffs. Each item is a serious problem that needs attention from

TABLE 2.2

Obvious Payoff Opportunities

- Excessive turnover of critical talent: 35% above benchmark data

- Very low market share in a market with few players

- Inadequate customer service: 3.89 on a 10-point customer satisfaction scale

- Safety record is among the worst in the industry

- This year's out-of-compliance fines total $1.2 million, up 82% from last year

- Excessive product returns: 30% higher than previous year

- Excessive absenteeism in call centers: 12.3%, compared to 5.4% industry average

- Sexual harassment complaints per 1,000 employees are the highest in the industry

- Grievances are up 38% from last year

- The cost to the city for each homeless person is $75,000

- Operating costs are 47% higher than industry average

executives, administrators, or politicians. To begin with a series of questions about the severity of the problem might insult the intelligence of the requestor or client. For these situations, it would be safe to move ahead to the business needs level rather than invest too much time and resources in analysis of the payoff. After the solution is defined, a forecast may be appropriate.

Not So Obvious Payoff Opportunities

In other proposed programs, however, the issues might be unclear or arise from political motives or biases. Table 2.3 shows opportunities for which the payoff is not as obvious. The opportunities that are not so obvious call for more detail. Some requests are common, as executives and administrators suggest a process change. The requests appear to have the program identified, but without a clear reason as to why. These types of requests could deliver substantial

TABLE 2.3

Not So Obvious Payoff Opportunities

- Improve leadership competencies for all managers.
- Organize a business development conference.
- Establish a project management office.
- Provide job training for unemployed workers.
- Train all team leaders on crucial conversations.
- Develop an "open-book" company.
- Become a technology leader.
- Create a great place to work.
- Implement a career advancement program.
- Create a wellness and fitness center.
- Build capability for future growth.
- Create an empowered workforce.
- Become a green company.
- Integrate all technology systems.
- Improve branding for all products.
- Implement lean Six Sigma for all professional employees.

value, but only if they are focused and clearly defined at the start. In our work at the ROI Institute, we have seen many vague requests turn into valuable programs. Sometimes overlooking the vague is a mistake; these requests can result in valuable contributions, as they can lead to critical analysis ensuring an appropriate focus on development.

The Cost of a Problem

Problems are sometimes expensive. To determine the cost of a problem, its potential consequences must be examined and converted to monetary values. Table 2.4 shows a list of potential costly problems. Most can easily be converted to money, and some already are. If a problem cannot be converted to money within the resources and time constraints of the project request, the problem is an intangible. For example, excessive carbon emissions from operating facilities is a serious problem, but it may not be one that can be converted to money, and thus result in a project to reduce the emissions. Time can easily be converted into money by calculating the fully loaded cost of the individual's time spent performing unproductive tasks. Employee turnover can be converted to money, based on the cost to replace the departing employee. Productivity problems, equipment damage, and equipment underuse are other examples of problems that have an apparent cost associated with them.

TABLE 2.4

Potentially Costly Problems

• Inventory shortages	• Employee dissatisfaction
• Excessive carbon emissions	• Productivity problems
• Excessive time	• Customer dissatisfaction
• Excessive employee turnover	• Inefficiencies
• Errors/mistakes	• Excessive conflicts
• Employee withdrawal	• Excessive direct costs
• Waste	• Tarnished image
• Accidents	• Equipment damage
• Delays	• Lack of coordination
• Excessive staffing	• Equipment underused
• Bottlenecks	• Excessive stress

Examining costs means examining *all* the costs and their implications. For example, the full costs of accidents include not only the cost of lost workdays and medical expenses, but also their effect on insurance premiums, the time required for investigations, damages to equipment, and the time of all employees who address the accident. The cost of a customer complaint includes the cost of the time to resolve the complaint, as well as the value of the item, fee, or service that is adjusted because of the complaint. The most important cost is the loss of future business and goodwill from the complaining customer, plus potential customers who become aware of the issue.

The Value of Opportunity

Just as the cost of a problem can be tabulated in most situations, the value of an opportunity can also be determined. Examples of opportunities include

- implementing a new process
- installing new technology
- upgrading the workforce for a more competitive environment.

In these situations, a problem may not exist, but a tremendous opportunity is available to move ahead of the competition if immediate action is taken. Properly placing a value on this opportunity requires considering possible consequences if the project or program is not pursued, and taking into account the windfall that might be realized by seizing the opportunity. The monetary value is derived by following the different scenarios to convert specific business impact measures to money. The challenge lies in ensuring a credible analysis. Forecasting the value of an opportunity involves many assumptions, whereas calculating the value of a known outcome is often grounded in a more credible analysis.

Final Thoughts

This step highlights the first level of needs assessments, payoff needs. Assessment of payoff needs is important because it helps verify that the potential project or program is worthy of implementation. It addresses the question very directly: "Is this a problem worth solving, or an opportunity worth pursuing?" This question is important to ask because many projects, unfortunately, are not worth pursuing, and some discussion or analysis may prevent the request from the very beginning. This step focuses on the types of questions that need to be asked to determine if the project should be pursued. They must be addressed very systematically and diplomatically to ensure there is a valid request. The next step focuses directly on the business issue which is business alignment.

Identify Business Needs

The third step in business alignment is to identify the business needs for the program or project. This step is closely linked to the previous step in the needs analysis, developing the payoff needs. To determine business needs, specific measures must be pinpointed so the business situation is clearly assessed. The term *business* is a broad term and is used in governments, nonprofits, educational institutions, and private sector organizations. Programs and projects in all types of organizations can show business contribution by improving productivity, quality, and efficiency, as well as by saving time and reducing costs.

Business Measures

A business need is represented by a business measure. Any process, item, or perception can be measured, and the measurement is critical to this level of analysis. If the program focuses on solving a problem, there must be a clear understanding of that problem and the measures that define it. The measures might also be obvious if the program prevents a problem. If the program takes advantage of a potential opportunity, the measures are usually there as well. If not, a clear, detailed description of the opportunity will help clarify the measure. The key is that measures are already in the system, ready to be captured for this level of analysis. The challenge is to define and find them economically and swiftly.

Business Measures Represented by Hard Data

Business measures are sometimes categorized by hard data and soft data. Distinguishing between the two types of data helps in the process of defining specific business measures. Hard data are primary measures of improvement presented in rational, undisputed facts that are usually accumulated. They are the most desired type of data because they're easy to measure and quantify, and relatively easy to convert to monetary values. The ultimate criteria for measuring the effectiveness of an organization are hard data such as revenue, productivity, profitability, cost control, and quality assurance.

Hard data are objectively based and represent common, credible measures of performance. They are usually divided into four categories, as shown in Table 3.1. These categories—output, quality, cost, and time—are typical performance measures in organizations, including private sector firms, government agencies, nongovernmental agencies, nonprofits, and educational institutions.

Output. Visible hard-data results from a program or project involve improvements in the output of the work unit, section, department, division, or entire organization. All organizations, regardless of type, must have basic measurements of output, such as the products sold, patients treated, students graduated, tons produced, or packages shipped. These items are monitored so changes can easily be measured by comparing before and after outputs. When programs are expected to drive an output measure, those knowledgeable about the situation can usually make estimates of output changes.

Quality. One of the most significant hard-data categories is quality. When quality is a major concern for an organization, processes are likely in place to measure and monitor it. Thanks in part to the rising popularity of quality improvement processes (e.g., total quality management, continuous quality improvement, and Six Sigma), pinpointing the correct quality measures—and in many cases placing a monetary value on them—has proven successful. Quality improvement program results can be documented using the standard cost of quality as a value.

Cost. Another important hard-data category is cost improvement. Many projects and programs are designed to lower, control, or eliminate the cost of a specific process or activity. Achieving these cost targets contributes immediately to the bottom line.

Some organizations have an extreme focus on cost reduction. Consider Wal-Mart, whose tagline is "Save Money. Live Better." Wal-Mart focuses on lowering costs on all processes and products, and also on passing the savings to customers. When direct cost savings are used, no efforts are necessary to convert data to monetary value because the costs themselves reflect this value. There can be as many cost items as there are accounts in a cost-accounting system. In addition, costs can be combined in any number of ways to develop the costs needed for a particular program or project.

Time. Time has become a critical measure for today's organizations. Some gauge performance almost exclusively on time. Consider FedEx, whose tagline is "The World on Time." When asked what business FedEx is in, the company's top executives say, "We engineer time." For FedEx, time is so critical that it defines success or failure. Time savings may mean that a program is completed faster than originally planned, a product is introduced earlier, or the time to restore a network is reduced. These savings can translate into lower costs.

TABLE 3.1

Examples of Hard Data

OUTPUT	QUALITY
• Completion rate	• Failure rates
• Units produced	• Dropout rates
• Tons manufactured	• Scrap
• Items assembled	• Waste
• Money collected	• Rejects
• Items sold	• Error rates
• New accounts generated	• Rework
• Forms processed	• Shortages
• Loans approved	• Product defects
• Inventory turnover	• Deviation from standard
• Patients visited	• Product failures
• Applications processed	• Inventory adjustments
• Students graduated	• Time card corrections
• Tasks completed	• Incidents
• Output per hour	• Compliance discrepancies
• Productivity	• Agency fees
• Work backlog	
• Incentive bonus	

Business Measures Represented by Soft Data

Hard data might lag behind changes and conditions in human performance within an organization by months; therefore, it is useful to supplement hard data with soft data such as attitude, motivation, and satisfaction. Often more difficult to collect and analyze, soft data are used when hard data are unavailable, or to

Table 3.1, continued

COSTS	TIME
• Shelter costs	• Cycle time
• Treatment costs	• Equipment downtime
• Budget variances	• Overtime
• Unit costs	• On-time shipments
• Cost by account	• Time to project completion
• Variable costs	• Processing time
• Fixed costs	• Set up time
• Overhead costs	• Time to proficiency
• Operating costs	• Learning time
• Program cost savings	• Meeting schedules
• Accident costs	• Repair time
• Program costs	• Efficiency
• Sales expense	• Work stoppages
• Participant costs	• Order response
	• Late reporting
	• Lost time days

supplement hard data. Soft data are also more difficult to convert to monetary values and are often based on subjective input. They are less credible as a performance measurement and tend to be behavior oriented, but represent important measures just the same. Table 3.2 shows common examples of soft data.

Work habits. Employee work habits are important to the success of work groups. Dysfunctional habits can lead to an unproductive work group, while productive work habits can boost the group's output and morale. Examples of work habits that might be difficult to measure or convert to monetary values appear in Table 3.2. The outcome of some work habits, including employee turnover,

TABLE 3.2

Examples of Soft Data

WORK HABITS

- Tardiness
- Visits to the dispensary
- Violations of safety rules
- Communication breakdowns
- Excessive breaks

WORK CLIMATE/SATISFACTION

- Grievances
- Discrimination charges
- Employee complaints
- Job satisfaction
- Organization commitment
- Employee engagement
- Employee loyalty
- Intent to leave
- Stress

CUSTOMER SERVICE

- Customer complaints
- Customer satisfaction
- Customer dissatisfaction
- Customer impressions
- Customer loyalty
- Customer retention
- Customer value
- Lost customers

EMPLOYEE DEVELOPMENT/ ADVANCEMENT

- Promotions

- Capability
- Intellectual capital
- Programs completed
- Requests for transfer
- Performance appraisal ratings
- Readiness
- Networking

CREATIVITY/INNOVATION

- Creativity
- Innovation
- New ideas
- Suggestions
- New products and services
- Trademarks
- Copyrights and patents
- Process improvements
- Partnerships
- Alliances

IMAGE

- Brand awareness
- Reputation
- Leadership
- Social responsibility
- Environmental friendliness
- Social consciousness
- Diversity
- External awards

absenteeism, and accidents, are in the hard-data category because they're easily converted to monetary values.

Work climate/satisfaction. Several measures reflect employee dissatisfaction. Complaints and grievances sometimes fall in the hard-data category because of their ease of conversion to money. However, most of the items are considered soft-data items. Job satisfaction, organizational commitment, and employee engagement show how attitudes shape the organization. Stress is often a byproduct of a fast-paced work climate. These issues and measurement of these issues are gaining prominence in most organizations.

Customer service. Because increased global competition fosters a greater need to serve and satisfy customers, more organizations are putting into place customer service measures that reflect customer satisfaction, loyalty, and retention. Few measures are as important as those linked to customers.

Employee development/advancement. Employees are routinely developed, assigned new jobs, and promoted. Many soft-data measures can indicate the consequences of crucial activities and processes, such as building capability, creating intellectual capital, enhancing readiness, and fostering networks.

Creativity/innovation. Creativity and innovation are key aspects of successful organizations. A variety of measures can be developed to show the creative spirit of employees and the related outcomes, such as ideas, suggestions, copyrights, patents, and products and services. While the collective creative spirit of employees might be a soft-data item, the outcomes of creativity and innovation qualify as hard data. Still, many executives consider innovation a soft-data item.

Image. Perhaps some of the softest measures relate to image. Executives attempt to increase brand awareness, particularly with sales and marketing programs. Reputation is another measure that is growing in importance. Organizations seek to improve their standings as good employers, good citizens, and good stewards of investors' money. Leadership is probably the most sought-after measure and is influenced by initiatives designed to build leadership within the organization. Image, social responsibility, environmental friendliness, and social consciousness are key outputs of a variety of programs and projects aimed at making the organization well rounded. Diversity is also important for many organizations, which focus programs on increasing diversity of ideas, products, people, and initiatives. Finally, external awards are the outcomes of many activities and programs. Some organizations invest in full-time employees to focus solely on applying for such awards. This particular measure represents the activity, support, and engagement of all employees, including the organization's leadership.

Tangible vs. Intangible Measures: A Better Approach

A challenge with regard to soft versus hard data is converting soft measures to monetary values. The key to this problem is to remember that, ultimately, all roads lead to hard data. Although creativity may be categorized as a form of soft data, a creative workplace can develop new products or new patents, which leads to greater revenue—clearly a hard data measure. Although it is possible to convert the measures to monetary amounts, it is often more realistic and practical to leave them in non-monetary form. This decision is based on considerations of credibility and the cost of the conversion.

According to the standards of the ROI methodology, an intangible measure is defined as a measure that is intentionally not converted to money. If a soft data measure can be converted to a monetary amount credibly using minimal resources, it is considered tangible, reported as a monetary value, and incorporated in the ROI calculation. If a data item cannot be converted to money credibly with minimal resources, it is listed as an intangible measure. Therefore, when defining business needs, the key difference between measures is not whether they represent hard or soft data, but whether they are tangible or intangible. In either case, they are important contributions toward the desired payoff and important business impact data.

Issues About Impact Measures

When assessing business impact measures, several issues must be considered. The impact data must first be collected in order to be assessed. In many situations, the impact data is in place, but a method of collecting it from the source must be determined. Collateral measures must be considered. These measures are positively or negatively influenced by the program, unintentionally. Finally, successive impact measures must be considered: What other measures will be subsequently affected as a direct result of the program's implementation?

Sources of Impact Data

Sources of impact data, whether hard or soft, are plentiful. They come from routine reporting systems within the organization. In many situations, these items have led to the need for the program or project. Table 3.3 shows a sampling of the vast array of documents, systems, databases, and reports that can be used to select the specific measure or measures to monitor throughout the program.

Some program planners and team members believe corporate data sources are scarce because the data are not readily available to them, near their workplace, or within easy reach through database systems. With a little determination and searching, however, the data can usually be identified. In our experience, more than 90 percent of the impact measures that matter to an organization have already been developed and are readily available in databases or systems. Rarely do new data collection systems or processes have to be developed.

Collateral Measures

When searching for the proper measures to connect to the program and pinpoint business needs, it's helpful to consider all the possible measures that could be influenced. Sometimes, collateral measures move in harmony with the program. For example, efforts

TABLE 3.3

Sources of Data

- Department records
- Work unit reports
- Human capital databases
- Payroll records
- Quality reports
- Design documents
- Manufacturing reports
- Test data
- Compliance reports
- Marketing data
- Sales records
- Service records
- Annual reports

- Safety and health reports
- Benchmarking data
- Industry/trade association data
- R&D status reports
- Suggestion system data
- Customer satisfaction data
- Project management data
- Cost data statements
- Financial records
- Scorecards
- Dashboards
- Productivity records
- Employee engagement data

to improve safety might also improve productivity and increase job satisfaction. Thinking about the adverse impact on certain measures also helps. For example, when cycle times are reduced, quality could suffer; or when sales increase, customer satisfaction could deteriorate. Program team members must prepare for these unintended consequences and capture them as relevant data items.

Successive Impact Measures

A potentially confusing issue is the fact that some impact measures have a successive chain of impact. The difficulty lies in deciding whether one measure is appropriate or if all measures are appropriate. For example, Table 3.4 details five possible consequences of sexual harassment in the workplace. The victim of the harassment suffers stress; the victim's job satisfaction drops; internal complaints of sexual harassment increase; the victim is increasingly absent from work; and employee turnover rises as victims seek employment elsewhere. The difficulty lies in determining which measures (if not all) are influenced by a sexual harassment prevention program. Most of this is sorted out in the up-front needs assessment to ensure that the particular program can indeed influence all these measures. Even if the principal focus of the program is to reduce complaints, it is important to determine whether the other measures are connected. If they are, they also could become objectives for the program.

When considering complaints, there is a successive series of impact measures. A formal internal complaint, if not resolved, could convert to an external charge with the Equal Employment

TABLE 3.4

Successive Impact Measures

Consequences of sexual harassment in the workplace can be successive.

Adapted from "Preventing Sexual Harassment—Healthcare Inc.," chapter 1, *Proving the Value of HR: ROI Case Studies*, 2nd ed. P.P. Phillips & J.J. Phillips. Birmingham, Alabama. ROI Institute, 2010.

Opportunity Commission. If that charge is not resolved to the victim's satisfaction, he or she has a right to sue the employer, creating a litigated complaint. Litigation leads to legal fees and expenses and also to settlements. Ultimately, all of this, from prevention to investigation to defense, represents a significant cost.

A program could actually have objectives for each of these. Although they should all improve in relative proportion, this might not be the case. Under U.S. law, employees have a right to sue an employer, even before an external charge is actually resolved or if it is resolved in favor of the victim. For those reasons, the focus might be on reducing the number of litigated complaints. The confusion comes when the monetary value of this program is calculated. Converting data to monetary value is critical to evaluation when an ROI calculation is pursued. Using all six impact measures represents a tremendous amount of duplication. It would be best to take one measure and use it in the conversion process. Still, they can all be objectives that are influenced by the sexual harassment prevention project. This series of successive impact measures can usually be uncovered when asking a series of "what if" questions. What if this measure happens? Does it lead to something else?

Final Thoughts

This step on identifying needs focused directly on the business measure. This third step to business alignment is critical because this is the potential measure for alignment, identifying actual business measures connected to the program. At this point in the analysis, it may only be perceived as being connected. The next two steps will connect this business need to the particular solution.

This step fully defines business measures, examining different categories that are common for grouping purposes. Soft data and hard data are typical categories of business data. Perhaps a more defined categorization is tangible versus intangible, while recognizing that all business measures can be converted to money credibly, at least with a reasonable amount of resources. The good news in this chapter is that the business measures are plentiful. They are already in the organization; they exist everywhere and the challenge is to connect them to the program.

Identify Performance Needs

OVERVIEW

There are a variety of analysis techniques to establish the reasons behind the current performance of a business measure.

Cost and time are two essential factors to consider when choosing which technique best suits your needs.

In the needs analysis process, this step explores reasons the business measure is at its present level rather than at the desired level of performance. This is step four for achieving business alignment. If the proposed program addresses a problem, this step focuses on the cause of the problem. If the program takes advantage of an opportunity, this step focuses on what is inhibiting the organization from reaching that opportunity.

Analysis Techniques

This step might require a variety of analytical techniques to uncover the causes of the problem or inhibitors to success. Table 4.1 shows a brief listing of techniques. It is important to relate the issue to the organizational setting, the behavior of the individuals involved, and the functioning of various systems. Analysis techniques often use tools from problem-solving, quality assurance, and performance improvement fields. Using multiple techniques is often important because measures are sometimes inhibited for several reasons.

TABLE 4.1

Analysis Techniques

• Diagnostic questionnaires	• Statistical process control
• Focus groups	• Brainstorming
• Probing interviews	• Problem analysis
• Job satisfaction surveys	• Cause-and-effect diagram
• Engagement surveys	• Force-field analysis
• Exit interviews	• Mind mapping
• Exit surveys	• Affinity diagrams
• Nominal group technique	• Simulations

The resources needed to examine records, research databases, and observe situations and individuals must be taken into account. Analysis takes time. The use of expert input, both internally and externally, can add to the cost and duration of the evaluation. The needs at this level can vary considerably and might include:

◆ ineffective behavior
◆ dysfunctional work climate
◆ inadequate systems
◆ disconnected process flow
◆ improper procedures
◆ unsupportive culture
◆ insufficient technology.

These needs must be uncovered using many of the methods listed in Table 4.1. When needs vary and techniques abound, the risk exists for excessive analysis and cost. Consequently, a sensible approach must be taken. Balance must exist between the level of analysis and availability of resources and time.

Questionnaires and Surveys

Questionnaires and surveys are probably the most common and inexpensive instruments used to collect data. Questionnaires come in all sizes, from brief reaction forms to detailed instruments. Questionnaires can be used to obtain all types of data, ranging from subjective information about employees' feelings, to business impact data for use in alignment. They are convenient for exploring the cause of problems. Here is an example that illustrates the power of a questionnaire: An office product firm was concerned about the lack of sales and market share growth. A questionnaire was sent to the sales team asking their perspective of what was inhibiting sales growth, the current level of customer loyalty, the strength of their competition, the challenges the organization was facing, and the outlook for the next year. In addition, the questionnaire prompted employees to give specific suggestions for improving sales, customer loyalty, and market share. This powerful questionnaire generated tremendous insight into the cause of the problem (e.g. lack of sales and market share growth).

Attitude surveys measure job satisfaction, organizational commitment, employee engagement, and a variety of other issues. While it is impossible to measure an attitude precisely because the input may not represent a respondent's true feelings, and attitudes tend to change with time, it is possible to obtain a reasonable assessment of employees' attitudes about work and the organization. Continuous measurements are required to show changes in attitudes. For example, some organizations are using a data collection process that taps the input of part or all of the employees through the use of very brief surveys. The particular problem is identified and is presented to the group through a quick and informal survey method. In one example, an upscale retail chain was experiencing an excessive turnover rate. Using eePulse, employees were asked five simple questions that required only a few minutes to respond. They were asked to identify the problems. The data was immediately fed back to the group, and additional questions were assembled.

The next week they were asked to react to additional questions. The results were then communicated to the group, along with proposed solutions. The solutions were rated the next week. Eventually this process continued until the best solutions were identified and action plans were put in place. This is an excellent way to tap the creative spirit of the group, the collaborative approach of the entire team, and use brief surveys in the process.

Interviews

Another helpful data collection method is the interview, although it is not used as frequently as questionnaires or surveys. A project team, other internal employees, or an outside third party can conduct interviews. Interviews can provide data that are not available in performance records or is difficult to obtain through written responses. Employees may be reluctant to provide input on a questionnaire, but will volunteer the information to a skillful interviewer who uses probing techniques to uncover changes in perceptions and attitudes.

Two basic types of interviews are structured and unstructured. Much like a questionnaire, the structured interview presents specific questions with little room to deviate from the desired responses. The unstructured interview is more flexible and can include probing for additional information. As important data are uncovered, a skilled interviewer can ask a few general questions that can lead to more detailed information.

One of the most utilized processes to uncover the causes of problems is the exit interview, taken just before or after an employee leaves the organization. Exit interviews can be face-to-face interviews, a questionnaire, a brief survey, or even a focus group. An anonymous questionnaire, administered confidentially, usually gets the best results for the costs.

Although exiting employees would seem to be the best source of data to determine why employees are leaving, exit interviews are notoriously inaccurate and unreliable; however, they need not be. When properly designed and implemented, they can provide excellent data to develop retention solutions. Three key issues represent challenges to conducting exit interviews.

♦ **The response rates may be low.** The rate of return may be very low. Departing employees don't feel obligated to provide data. The last thing they may want to do is help the organization after they have decided to leave.

♦ **The data may be incomplete or inaccurate.** Even when employees respond to the questions, their responses may not be complete or accurate. Since they are no longer attached to the organization, they may be unwilling to devote much time to this issue. Consequently, their responses are short, incomplete, and sporadic.

♦ **Data may be purposely biased.** For fear of retaliation or negative references, the employee may provide misleading input. An employee may indicate that working conditions were fine, but that he or she received an offer that could not be refused, when that might not be the case.

STEP 4

These issues pose critical challenges when conducting exit interviews.

Two major disadvantages of the interview are that it is time-consuming and there is little sense of anonymity. Also, interviewers must be trained to ensure that the process is consistent across respondents. The primary advantage is that the interview process ensures that a question is answered and that the interviewer understands the responses. Also, the interview allows for probing to uncover more details.

Focus Groups

A focus group is a small group discussion conducted by an experienced facilitator. It is designed to solicit qualitative judgments on a planned topic or issue. An extension of the interview, focus groups are particularly helpful when in-depth feedback and probing are required. Group members are all required to provide their input, as individual input builds on group input.

A focus group strategy has several advantages. The basic premise is that when judgments are subjective, several individual judgments are better than one. Thus, the group process in which participants often motivate one another is an effective method for generating new ideas and hypotheses. It is inexpensive and can be quickly planned and conducted. Its flexibility makes it possible to explore a variety of issues.

Perhaps one of the most useful and productive tools to determine the causes of turnover is to use a focus group process called the nominal group technique. With this process, a group of employees are asked to provide information on why their colleagues behave a particular way. The key issue is to focus on the reasons why others would exhibit specific behaviors and not why they, themselves would. This repositions the data collection from a potentially threatening to a non-threatening environment. The recommended audience is a representative sample of the target groups experiencing the behaviors. The group size of each sample should be eight to 12. A small number of samples would be appropriate for large target groups. The total sample size needed for statistical validity depends on several factors and can be accurately determined. However, this number may become expensive and unnecessary. One approach is to sample until trends and patterns begin to emerge. For example, in a target group with a thousand employees doing the same job, five to 10 samples would probably be sufficient. The key issue is to examine the results to confirm a pattern. Although the group process is inexpensive compared to some techniques, the issue may represent a balance of economics versus accuracy. An example will illustrate the power of the nominal group technique.

Southeast Corridor Bank (SCB), a regional bank operating in four states, had grown from a single state operation to a multi-state network through a progressive and strategic campaign of acquisitions. As with many organizations, SCB faced merger and integration problems, including excessive employee turnover. SCB's annual turnover rate was 57 percent, compared to an industry average of 26 percent. The new senior vice president for human resources faced several important challenges when he joined SCB. Among them was the need to reduce turnover. Although management was not aware of the full impact of turnover, they knew it was causing operational problems, taking up much staff and supervisor time, and creating disruptive situations with customers.

The nominal group technique was selected to analyze the cause of turnover because it allowed unbiased input to be collected efficiently and accurately across the organization. A focus group was planned with 12 employees in each region for a total of six groups representing all six regions. In addition, two focus groups were planned for the clerical staff in corporate headquarters. This approach provided approximately a 10 percent sample and was considered to be a sufficient number to pinpoint the problem. Participants for focus groups represented areas where turnover was highest. They described why their colleagues were leaving—not why they would leave themselves. Input was solicited from participants in a carefully structured format, using third party facilitators. The data were integrated and weighted so that the most important reasons were clearly identified. This process has the advantages of low cost, high reliability, and being unbiased. Data were captured in a two-hour meeting in each regional location. Only two days of external facilitator time was necessary to collect and summarize data for review.

The nominal group technique unfolds quickly in 10 steps.
1. The process is briefly described along with a statement of confidentiality. The importance of participant input is underscored and participants understand what they must do and what it means to SCB.
2. On a piece of paper, participants are asked to make a list of specific reasons why they feel their colleagues have left SCB or why others may leave in the future. It is very important for the question to reflect the actions or potential actions of others, although their comments will

probably reflect their own views (and that is what is actually needed).

3. In a round robin format, each person reveals one reason at a time and it is recorded on flip chart paper. At this point, no attempts are made to integrate the issues; just record the data on paper. It is important to understand the issue and fully describe it on paper. The lists are placed on the walls so that when this step is complete, as many as 50 or 60 items are listed and visible.

4. The next step is to consolidate and integrate the lists. Some of the integration is easy because the items may contain the same words and meaning. For others, it is important to ensure that the meanings for the cause of the turnover are the same, before they are consolidated. When integrated, the remaining list may contain 30 or 40 different reasons for turnover.

5. Participants are asked to review all of the items, and carefully select which ten items they consider to be the most important causes and list them individually on index cards. At first, participants are not concerned about which cause is number one, but are instructed to simply list the 10 most important ones on the cards. Participants usually realize that their original list was not complete or accurate, and they will pick up other issues for this list.

6. Participants sort the ten items by order of importance, the number one item being the most important, and number 10, the least important.

7. In a round robin format, each participant reveals a cause of turnover, starting from the top. Each participant reveals his or her number one item, and 10 points are recorded on the flip chart paper next to the item. The next participant reveals the number one issue and so on until the entire group offers the top cause for turnover. Next, the number two reason is identified, and nine points are recorded on the flip chart paper next to the item. This process continued until all cards have been revealed and points recorded.

8. The numbers next to each item are totaled. The item with the most points becomes the number one cause of turnover. The one with the second most points becomes the second cause of turnover and so on. The top 15 causes are then captured from the group and are reported as the weighted average cause of turnover from that group.

9. This process was completed for all six regional groups and the clerical staff groups. Trends began to emerge quickly from one group to the other. The actual raw scores from each group were combined for the integration of the six regional focus groups.

10. The actual raw scores were then combined to integrate the results of the six regional focus groups and the clerical group.

The following list in Table 4.2 shows the 10 most important reasons for turnover in the bank branches.

TABLE 4.2

Specific Needs

1. Lack of opportunity for advancement

2. Lack of opportunity to learn new skills and new product knowledge

3. Pay level not adequate

4. Not enough responsibility and empowerment

5. Lack of recognition and appreciation of work

6. Lack of teamwork in the branch

7. Lack of preparation for customer service problems

8. Unfair and unsupportive supervisor

9. Too much stress at peak times

10. Not enough flexibility in work schedules

Recognizing that not all the causes of turnover could be addressed immediately, the bank's management set out to work on the top five reasons while it considered a variety of options. Eventually, a skill-based pay system was created. The program was designed to expand the scope of the jobs, with increases in pay for acquiring skills, and to provide a clear path for advancement and improvement. Jobs were redesigned from narrowly focused teller duties to an expanded job with a new title: The tellers all became banking representative I, II, or III.

Brainstorming

Brainstorming is perhaps the most widely recognized technique to encourage creative thinking. It has become an important tool for generating the causes of organizational issues. The process facilitation is similar to that for a focus group and those design issues and guidelines also apply to the brainstorming session. The goal is to generate as many ideas as possible with no restrictions. The groups are best kept small, usually in range of six to 12 participants. The group should focus on the actual problem.

The individuals invited to participate should be those who best understand the problem and are in a position to know the causes and corresponding potential solutions. The group should have a complete understanding of the problems, issues, and challenges. Providing information in advance will help the individuals develop ideas prior to the meeting.

The ground rules for the process are fairly straightforward:
- Individuals are encouraged to offer as many ideas as possible.
- The ideas are not criticized by anyone, regardless of how they may be perceived.
- All ideas are recorded.
- All participants should have ample time to share their ideas.
- Freewheeling is encouraged, even if the ideas seem to be off the wall.

When input ceases to be productive, a variety of techniques are available to stimulate additional creativity and ideas. Three are very helpful:

◆ The participation is rotated through the group to enable one individual to build off the ideas of another. This also provides ample time for reflection from those who are not directly participating.

◆ Using the concept of idea building, individuals are encouraged to add to or expand on previous ideas or to offer similar or even alternate issues as ideas.

◆ Quiet periods can help people reflect and think through the problem, sifting through the data mentally and generating additional ideas. This period could last up to half an hour before it becomes pointless.

The data can be summarized in a variety of ways. Eliminating items, combining items, and reaching consensus on items are key steps in the process.

Cause-and-Effect Model

The cause-and-effect model is very useful for repetitive issues. This process can be used to create what is sometimes called the fishbone diagram because of its appearance, as shown in Figure 4.1. The process follows the focus group and brainstorming formats, except the major categories of causes are identified first, with minor causes added. The minor cause categories, which can be considerable, are provided by the group using idea-generating processes. Here, the focus is more specific and the group must be knowledgeable about the problem so that they can offer minor causes of the problem. The steps are very simple:

1. The groups are selected based on their capability to provide insight into the causes of the problem.

2. The groups are provided instructions and their role in the process is outlined.

3. The major cause categories are either identified or offered. They are offered if there is previous information to indicate

FIGURE 4.1

Example of a Fishbone Diagram

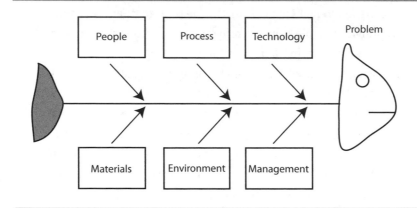

the specific cause (from exit interviews or other data-collection methods).

4. After some discussion, the most likely causes are circled. This is only after each item is critically evaluated and the group has reached a consensus as to which causes are most relevant. This process is more focused and, therefore, is more likely to help the group find the real cause for a problem.

5. With the major cause categories clearly identified and entered on the diagram, the group members are asked to indicate the minor causes related to each major cause category. These can be listed as minor causes, or sometimes just the "why" for the particular major cause category.

6. The fishbone diagram is then completed, showing the major and minor causes for the problem.

Other Tools

A variety of other tools are available, primarily from the quality and performance improvement process, which can be used to analyze the cause of the problem. Listed here are five that might be helpful:

Force field analysis is a visual tool for analyzing the different elements that resist change (restraining forces), and those elements that wish for change (facilitating forces). This is a useful technique to drive improvement and retention by developing plans to overcome the restraining forces and make maximum use out of the facilitating forces.

Mind mapping is an unstructured cause-and-effect analysis tool primarily designed for taking notes and solving problems. The problem is written on the center of a piece of paper and members of the group offer their suggestions or ideas as to the causes. These causes are drawn from the center as legs or lines. Branches are added to a line as additional causes or sub-causes are generated. This is similar to the cause-and-effect process, but might be more helpful with those individuals familiar with the mind-mapping process.

Affinity diagrams are used to collect input from groups and organize it according to the natural relationships between items. This technique has a conceptual and logical simplicity that allows for a clear view of the largest and most complex problems. Basically, it is a way to structure and classify vague ideas. Consequently, it is helpful when there is a need to focus on a complex, multi-faceted problem, such as turnover.

Relationship diagrams are used when there is a need to build a map of the logical, sequential links among items that are interconnected and related to a central problem, such as turnover. It facilitates the solution of problems when causes interact by dividing a problem into its basic components and isolating the relationships. The basic logic behind this tool is the same as that behind the cause-and-effect diagram.

Tree-shaped diagrams systematically outline the complete spectrum, paths, and tests that must be carried out in order to achieve a particular goal, such as business alignment. The use of this tool changes some generalities into details by isolating the intermediate conditions that must be satisfied. The diagram leads to identification of the more appropriate procedures and methods to solve the problem.

These and other techniques may be helpful for analyzing causes and relationships between causes. The important point is to use a tool that works best for the organization in a specific setting.

Final Thoughts

This chapter provides some of the tools necessary to take step four toward achieving business alignment: identify performance needs. This critical step points to a solution in the form of a project or program that will improve the business measure identified as a business need. When a business measure is not performing as well as it should, or there is an opportunity for improvement, the key issue is to find out what is inhibiting the measure, or what is causing it to be less effective than it should be. This requires an analysis of the cause by people involved with it. A variety of techniques are available and some of the most common ones are presented in this step. It is essential to make sure the right solution for the problem is appropriate for the opportunity. Step five focuses on identifying learning and preference needs.

Identify Learning and Preference Needs

Learning and preference needs must be identified, as they indirectly affect the business measures.

Learning measures focus on knowledge, skills, and attitudes. Preference needs drive the program features and requirements, according to the statements of individuals involved in the program.

The fifth step to business alignment is to identify the learning and preference needs. The needs assessment would not be complete without these last two levels, learning needs and preference needs. Although these levels do not directly reflect business measures, they indirectly affect them. Learning needs define the particular knowledge, skill, or information that must be acquired to satisfy the performance needs. Preference needs define how the various stakeholders—including the participants—prefer to have the solution implemented. These two levels of needs round out the needs assessment phase of the alignment process.

The Importance of Learning and Preference

For the learning and development function, learning needs assessment has sometimes been the only needs assessment conducted, essentially assuming that a request for a particular project or

STEP
5

program was a learning solution. Clearly, that is not the case, as we will show in this chapter. If it is a learning solution, the learning needs will define what that solution should look like. If it is not a learning solution, the learning needs will identify the knowledge and information component for the solution.

The preference needs are often not explored, assuming that these needs will be met or dictated by someone else. However, a project can come to a screeching halt if those involved do not see a need for it, or do not see it as valuable to their own success. Preferences need to be clearly defined and ultimately translated into reaction objectives. In short, these two levels of needs assessment not only round out the five levels of needs, they are also essential to ensure the proposed solution actually drives the business measure and achieves the highest possible level of success.

Learning Needs

Addressing the job performance needs uncovered in the previous step often requires specific knowledge, such as participants and team members learning how to perform a task differently or how to use a new process. In some cases, learning is the principal solution, as in competency development, major technology changes, capability development, quality processes, and system installations.

For other programs, learning is a minor part of the solution and involves simply understanding processes, procedures, and policies. For example, when a new ethics policy is implemented, the learning component requires understanding how the policy works and the participants' role in the policy. In short, a learning solution is not always needed. But all solutions have a learning component. A variety of approaches measure specific learning needs. Multiple tasks and jobs are usually found in a program, and each should be addressed separately.

Typical Measurement Categories

Learning measures focus on knowledge, skills, and attitudes, as well as confidence to apply or implement the program or process as desired. Sometimes, learning measures are expanded to different categories. Table 5.1 shows the typical measures collected at this level. Obviously, the more detailed the skills, the greater the number of objectives. Programs can vary, ranging from one or two simple skills to massive programs that may involve hundreds of skills.

Knowledge often includes the assimilation of facts, figures, and concepts. Instead of knowledge, the terms awareness, understanding, or information may be specific categories. Sometimes, perceptions or attitudes may change based on what a participant has learned. For example, in a diversity program, the participants' attitudes toward having a diverse work group often change with the implementation of the program; sometimes, the desire is to develop a reservoir of knowledge and skills and tap into it when developing capability, capacity, or readiness. When individuals are capable, they are often described as being job-ready.

An appropriate measure of learning might be the confidence that the participants have to use skills in their job settings for the first time. This becomes critical in job situations where skills must be performed accurately and to a certain standard. Sometimes, networking is part of a program and developing contacts that may be valuable later is important. This may be within, or external to, an organization. For example, a leadership development program may

TABLE 5.1

Typical Learning Measurement Categories

• Skills	• Information	• Capacity
• Knowledge	• Perception	• Readiness
• Awareness	• Attitudes	• Confidence
• Understanding	• Capability	• Contracts

include participants from different functional areas of the organization and an expected outcome, from a learning perspective, is to know who to contact at particular times in the future.

Subject Matter Experts

One of the most important approaches to determining learning needs is to ask those who understand the process. They can best determine what skills and knowledge are necessary to address the performance needs defined in the previous chapter. Then it might be possible to understand how much knowledge and how many skills already exist.

Job and Task Analysis

A job and task analysis offers a systematic look at information when a new job is created or when tasks within an existing job description change significantly. Essentially, the analysis collects and evaluates work-related information, determining specific knowledge, skills, tools, and conditions necessary to perform a particular job. The primary objective of the analysis is to collect information about the scope, responsibilities, and tasks related to a particular job or new set of responsibilities. In the context of developing learning needs, this information helps in preparing job profiles and job descriptions. These descriptions, in turn, serve as a platform for linking job requirements to specific information or training needs.

Performing a job and task analysis not only helps individuals who will use the program develop a clear picture of their responsibilities, but it also indicates what is expected of them. The amount of time needed to complete a job and task analysis varies from a few days to several months, depending on the complexity of the program. Components include identifying high performers, preparing a job analysis questionnaire, and developing other materials as necessary to collect information. During the job analysis, responsibilities are defined, tasks are detailed, and specific learning requirements are identified.

STEP **5**

Observations

Current practices within an organization might have to be observed to understand the context where the program is implemented. This technique can provide insight into the level of capability, as well as appropriate procedures. Observation is an established and respected data-collection method that can examine workflow and interpersonal interactions, including those between management and team members.

Sometimes, the observer is placed in the work environment specifically to observe others, but the observation is unknown to those being observed. In other instances, the observer previously worked in the environment, but is now in a different role. Another possibility is that the observer is invisible to those being observed. Examples include retail store mystery shopping, audio and video observation in a casino, and audio observation in a call center. It is important to remember that observation can uncover what individuals need to know or do as a program changes.

Demonstrations

In some situations, having employees demonstrate their abilities to perform a certain task or procedure provides valuable insight. The demonstration can be as simple as a skill practice or role play, or as complex as an extensive mechanical or electronic simulation. From this determination of job knowledge, specific learning needs can evolve.

Tests

Testing is not used as frequently as other needs assessment methods, but it can prove to be highly useful. Employees are tested to find out what they know about a particular situation. Test results help guide learning issues. For example, in one hospital chain, management was concerned that employees were unaware of the company's policy on sexual harassment or what actions constitute sexual harassment. In the early stages of the program analysis, a group of supervisors and managers, the target audience for the program, took a 20-item test about their knowledge of the sexual harassment policy (10 items) and knowledge about sexual harassment actions (10 items). The test scores revealed where insufficient knowledge existed and formed the basis of a program to reduce the number of sexual harassment complaints.

Management Assessment

When implementing programs in organizations in which there are existing managers or team leaders, input from the management team might be used to assess the current situation and the knowledge and skills that the new situation requires. This input can be collected through surveys, interviews, or focus groups. It can be a rich source of information about what the users of a new program would need to know to make it a success.

Where the learning component is minor, learning needs are simple. Determining specific learning needs can be time consuming for major programs for which new procedures, technologies, and processes are developed. As in the previous step, it is important not to spend excessive time analyzing at this early stage in the process, but collecting as much data as possible with minimal resources.

Preference Needs

This level of needs analysis drives the program features and requirements. Essentially, individuals prefer certain processes, schedules, or activities for the learning and performance improvement project. Those preferences define how the particular program will be implemented.

Typical preference needs are statements that define the parameters of the program in terms of timing, content, staffing, location, technology, and extent of disruption allowed. Table 5.2 shows the typical statements that reflect preferences. Although everyone involved has certain needs or preferences for the program, implementation is based on the input of several stakeholders rather than that of an individual. For example, participants involved in the program (those who must make it work) might have a particular preference, but their preference could exceed resources, time, and budget requirements. The immediate manager's input may help minimize the amount of disruption and maximize resources. Available funds are also a constraining resource. The urgency for program implementation may create a constraint in the preferences. Those who support or own the program often place preferences around the program in terms of timing, budget, and the use of technology. Because this is a Level 1 need, the program structure and solution will directly relate to the reaction objectives and to the initial reaction to the program.

STEP **5**

TABLE 5.2

Typical Preference Measurement Categories

• Ready	• Powerful	• Intent to use
• Useful	• Leading edge	• Planned action
• Necessary	• Just enough	• New information
• Appropriate	• Just for me	• Overall evaluation
• Motivational	• Efficient	• Content
• Rewarding	• Easy/difficult	• Method
• Practical	• Service-related	• Facilities/environment
• Valuable	• Relevance	• Facilitator/team leader evaluation
• Timely	• Importance	• Recommend to others
• Location	• Costs	• Duration
• Scope	• Delivery	• Audience

Many topics serve as targets for preference needs, because so many issues and processes are involved in a typical project or program. Preference is important for almost every major issue, step, or process to make sure outcomes are successful. Table 5.2 shows typical issues for preference. The list reveals possible needs of a project or program, beginning with readiness and moving through a variety of content-related issues to recommendations to others.

Final Thoughts

This step describes some of the key concepts of the last two levels of needs assessment, learning needs and preference needs. Together they round out and sometimes even define the solution if a learning and development program is needed. In a non-learning solution, the learning component is defined and various stakeholders' preferred perception of the solution is detailed. Preference needs are critical because they speak to the personal values of the individuals involved. If they are not clearly defined, the objectives will not be properly developed and those particular needs may not be met. The next step addresses developing objectives at all five levels.

Set Higher Levels of Objectives

OVERVIEW

Objectives must be set for achieving positive reaction from stakeholders, for ensuring participants have learned what's required, for completing what's expected in performance, for improving business impact measures, and for receiving the expected payoff and return on investment.

Objectives are powerful in that they provide direction, focus, and guidance.

The sixth step to business alignment is to set higher levels of objectives, specifically application and impact objectives. This step is noteworthy because it is the higher level of objectives

STEP 6

(particularly at business impact) that position programs to achieve business alignment. These objectives provide the direction and guidance for all individuals involved in the program. Setting higher levels of objectives keeps business alignment alive and on track during the project. However, to have business impact objectives, objectives at reaction, learning, application, and even ROI must be set, as shown in Table 6.1. This chapter briefly shows what's involved in developing objectives at all levels.

Reaction Objectives

For any project to be successful, various stakeholders must react to the project favorably, or at least not negatively. Ideally, the stakeholders should be satisfied with the project since the best project solutions offer win-win outcomes for the both client and

TABLE 6.1

Multiple Levels of Objectives

Levels of Objectives	Focus of Objectives
Level 1 Reaction	Defines a specific level of reaction to the project as it is revealed and communicated to the stakeholders
Level 2 Learning	Defines specific levels of knowledge, information, and skills as the stakeholders learn how to make the project successful.
Level 3 Application and Implementation	Defines specific measures and levels of success with application and implementation of project
Level 4 Impact	Defines the specific levels business measures will change or improve as a result of the project's implementation
Level 5 ROI	Defines the specific return on investment from the project, comparing costs against monetary benefits from the project

consultant. The stakeholders are those who are directly involved in implementing the project. This diverse group can consist of the employees who are involved in implementing the work, team leaders who are responsible for the changed process, customers who must use a redesigned product, suppliers who must follow a new system, citizens who must use a new procedure, or volunteers who must adjust to a new process. Stakeholders could also be managers who must support or assist the project in some way. Stakeholder reaction should be collected routinely through the project so that the feedback can be used to make adjustments, keep the project on track, and perhaps even redesign certain parts of it. Reaction objectives are necessary to maintain proper focus. Unfortunately, many projects do not have specific objectives at this level and data collection mechanisms are not put in place to ensure appropriate feedback for making needed adjustments. Table 6.2 presents typical reaction objectives.

TABLE 6.2

Typical Reaction Objectives

At the end of the program, participants should rate each of the following statements at least a 4 out of 5 on a 5-point scale:

- The program was organized.

- The facilitators were effective.

- The program was valuable for my work.

- The program was important to my success.

- The program was motivational for me personally.

- The program had practical content.

- The program contained new information.

- The program represented an excellent use of my time.

- I will use the material from this program.

Learning Objectives

Almost every project will involve a learning objective. In some cases that involve learning solutions, major change projects, and new technology implementations, the learning component is quite significant. To ensure that the various stakeholders have learned what's required in order to make the project successful, learning objectives are developed. Learning objectives are critical because they communicate expected outcomes from the learning component of the project, and they define the desired competence or the required performance to make the project successful. These objectives provide a basis for evaluating the learning since they often reflect the type of measurement process. Learning objectives should clearly indicate what participants must learn — sometimes with precision.

The three types of learning objectives are often defined as:
- ◆ awareness—familiarity with terms, concepts, and processes

- knowledge—general understanding of concepts, processes, or procedures
- performance—ability to demonstrate skills at least on a basic level.

The best learning objectives describe the behaviors that are observable and measurable, which are necessary for success with the project. They are often outcome-based, clearly worded, and specific. They specify what the particular stakeholder must know and do to implement the project successfully. Learning objectives can have three components:

- performance—what the participant or stakeholder will be able to do as a result of the project
- conditions under which the participant or stakeholder will perform the various tasks and processes
- criteria—the degree or level of proficiency necessary to perform a new task, process, or procedure that is part of the solution.

Table 6.3 shows some typical learning objectives. These objectives are critical to measuring learning. They communicate the expected outcomes of learning and define the desired competence or performance necessary for program success.

Application Objectives

As a project is implemented, it should be guided by application objectives that define clearly what is expected and often to what level of performance. Application objectives reflect the action desired from the project. They also involve particular milestones, indicating specifically when steps or phases of the process are completed. Application objectives are critical because they describe the expected outcomes in the intermediate area, that is, between learning what is necessary to make the project successful, and the actual impact that will be improved because of it. Application objectives describe how participants should perform, the process steps that should be taken, or technology that should be used as the project is implemented. The emphasis of application objectives is on action.

TABLE 6.3

Typical Learning Objectives

After completing the program, participants will be able to:

- Identify the six features of the new ethics policy.

- Demonstrate the use of each software routine in the standard time.

- Use problem-solving skills, given a specific problem statement.

- Determine whether they are eligible for the early retirement program.

- Score 75 or better in 10 minutes on the new-product quiz.

- Demonstrate all five customer-interaction skills with a success rating of 4 out of 5.

- Explain the five categories for the value of diversity in a work group.

- Document suggestions for award consideration.

- Score at least 9 out of 10 on a sexual harassment policy quiz.

- Identify five new technology trends explained at the conference.

- Name the six pillars of the division's new strategy.

- Successfully complete the leadership simulation in 15 minutes.

The best application objectives identify behaviors that are observable and measurable, or action steps in a process that can easily be observed or measured. They specify what the various stakeholders will change or have changed as a result of the project. As with learning objectives, application objectives may have three components: performance, condition, and criteria.

Table 6.4 shows typical application objectives and key questions asked at this level. Application objectives have almost always been included to some degree in projects, but have not been as specific as they could be or need to be. To be effective, they must clearly define the environment where the project is successfully implemented.

TABLE 6.4

Application Objectives

Typical Questions for Application Objectives

- What new or improved knowledge will be applied to the job?

- What is the frequency of skill application?

- What specific new task will be performed?

- What new steps will be implemented?

- What new procedures will be implemented or changed?

- What new guidelines will be implemented?

- Which meetings need to be held?

- Which tasks, steps, or procedures will be discontinued?

Typical Application Objectives

When the project is implemented:

- At least 99.1 percent of software users will be following the correct sequences after three weeks of use.
- Within one year, 10 percent of employees will submit documented suggestions for saving costs.
- The average 360-degree leadership assessment score will improve from 3.4 to 4.1 on a 5-point scale in 90 days.
- 95 percent of high-potential employees will complete individual development plans within two years.
- Employees will routinely use problem-solving skills when faced with a quality problem.
- Sexual harassment activity will cease within three months after the zero-tolerance policy is implemented.
- 80 percent of employees will use one or more of the three cost-containment features of the health care plan in the next six months.
- 50 percent of conference attendees follow up with at least one contact from the conference within 60 days.
- By November, pharmaceutical sales reps will communicate adverse effects of a specific prescription drug to all physicians in their territories.
- Managers will initiate three workout projects within 15 days.
- Sales and customer service representatives use all five interaction skills with at least half the customers within the next month.

STEP **6**

Impact Objectives

Almost every project should have impact objectives, even in the public sector and among nonprofits and non-government organizations. Business impact objectives are expressed in the key business measures that should be improved as the application objectives are achieved. The impact objectives are critical to measuring business performance because they define business-unit performance that should be connected to the project or program. They place emphasis on achieving bottom-line results that key client groups expect and demand. Finally, they ensure business alignment throughout the project or program.

TABLE 6.5

Typical Business Impact Objectives

After project completion, the following conditions should be met:

- After nine months, grievances should be reduced from three per month to no more than two per month at the Golden Eagle tire plant.

- The average number of new accounts should increase from 300 to 350 per month in six months.

- Tardiness at the Newbury Foundry should decrease by 20 percent within the next calendar year.

- An across-the-board reduction in overtime should be realized for front-of-house managers at Tasty Time restaurants in the third quarter of this year.

- Employee complaints should be reduced from an average of three per month to an average of one per month at Guarantee Insurance headquarters.

- By the end of the year, the average number of product defects should decrease from 214 per month to 153 per month at all Amalgamated Rubber extruding plants in the Midwest region.

- The company-wide employee engagement index should rise by one point during the next calendar year.

- Sales expenses for all titles at Proof Publishing Company should decrease by 10 percent in the fourth quarter.

- There should be a 10 percent increase in Pharmaceuticals, Inc. brand awareness among physicians during the next two years.

- Customer returns per month should decline by 15 percent in six months.

The best impact objectives contain data that are easily collected and are well known to the client group. They are results-based, clearly worded, and specify what the stakeholders have ultimately accomplished in the business unit as a result of the project.

The four major categories of hard data impact objectives are output, quality, cost, and time. Major categories of soft data impact objectives are customer service, work climate, and image. Typical measures that frame the objectives are presented in Step 3. Table 6.5 shows examples of impact objectives.

Return on Investment Objectives

A fifth level of objectives for projects is the expected return on investment. These objectives define the expected payoff from the project and compare the cost of it with the monetary benefits from the project.

This is the traditional financial ROI. The comparison is expressed as a percentage when the fractional values are multiplied by 100. In formula form, the ROI is:

$$\text{ROI (\%)} = \frac{\text{Net Program Benefits}}{\text{Program Costs}} \times 100$$

Net benefits are program benefits minus costs. This formula is essentially the same as the ROI for capital investments. For example, when a firm builds a new plant, the ROI is developed by dividing annual earnings by the investment. The annual earnings are comparable to net benefits (annual benefits minus the cost). The investment is comparable to fully loaded program costs, which represent the investment in the program.

An ROI of 50 percent means that the costs are recovered and an additional 50 percent of the costs are reported as "earnings." A program ROI of 150 percent indicates that the costs have been recovered and an additional 1.5 times the costs are captured as "earnings."

Here is an example to illustrate the ROI calculation: Public and private sector groups have been concerned about literacy and have developed a variety of programs to tackle the issue. Magnavox Electronics Systems Company was involved in one literacy program that focused on language and math skills for entry-level electrical and mechanical assemblers. The ROI objective was 25 percent. The results of the program were impressive. Productivity and quality alone yielded an annual value of $321,600. The fully loaded costs for the program were just $38,233. Thus, the return on investment was:

$$\text{ROI (\%)} = \frac{\$321,600 - \$38,233}{\$38,233} \times 100 = 741\%$$

For each dollar invested, Magnavox received $7.41 in return after the costs of the literacy program had been recovered.

Using the ROI formula essentially places program investments on a level playing field with other investments using the same formula and similar concepts. The ROI calculation is easily understood by key management and financial executives who regularly use ROI with other investments.

For many projects, the ROI objective is larger than what might be expected from the ROI of other expenditures—such as the purchase of a new company, a new building, or major equipment—but the two are related. For example, if the expected ROI from the purchase of a new company is 20 percent, the ROI from a project might be set at the 25 percent range. The important point is that the ROI objective should be established up front in discussions with the client.

Specific ROI Objectives

Specific objectives for ROI should be developed before an evaluation study is undertaken. While no generally accepted standards exist, four strategies have been used to establish a minimum acceptable requirement, or hurdle rate, for ROI in a program. The first approach is to set the ROI using the same values used to invest in capital expenditures, such as equipment, facilities, and new companies. For North America, Western Europe, and most of the Asia Pacific area (including Australia and New Zealand), the cost of capital is quite low, and this internal hurdle rate for ROI is usually in the 15 to 20 percent range. Using this strategy, organizations would set the expected ROI at the same value expected from other investments.

A second strategy is to use an ROI minimum that represents a higher standard than the value required for other investments. This target value is above the percentage required for other types of investments. The rationale: The ROI process for programs is still relatively new and often involves subjective input, including estimations. Because of that, a higher standard is required or suggested. For most areas in North America, Western Europe, and the Asia Pacific area, this value is set at 25 percent.

A third strategy is to set the ROI value at a break-even point. A 0 percent ROI represents break-even. The rationale for this approach is an eagerness to recapture the cost of the program only. This is the ROI objective for many public sector organizations. If the funds expended for programs can be captured, value and benefit have come from the program through the intangible measures (which are not converted to monetary values), and the behavior change that is evident in the application and implementation data. Thus, some organizations will use a break-even point, under the philosophy that they are not attempting to make a profit from a particular program.

Finally, a fourth, and sometimes recommended, strategy is to let the client or program sponsor set the minimum acceptable ROI value. In this scenario, the individual who initiates, approves, sponsors, or supports the program establishes the acceptable ROI. Almost every program has a major sponsor, and that person may be willing to offer the acceptable value. This links the expectations of financial return directly to the expectations of the individual sponsoring the program.

The Power of Objectives

Objectives are powerful in that they provide direction, focus, and guidance. They create interest, commitment, expectations, and satisfaction. Their effect on different stakeholders varies; they are a necessity, not a luxury. While the power of objectives at the reaction and learning levels is evident, the importance of objectives at higher levels requires additional explanation.

Application/Impact Objectives Drive Programs

Objectives at application and impact levels are routinely omitted from projects and programs. Ironically, these objectives are the most powerful as they focus on success with application and the corresponding outcomes. More specifically, they fuel a program or project by providing:

◆ focus and meaning to the program
◆ direction to the stakeholders
◆ definitions of success.

Application/Impact Objectives Enhance Design and Development

A risk not worth taking is sending vague objectives to a program designer or developer. Designers are creative, using their imaginations to build program content. Without clear, specific direction, they will insert their own assumptions regarding the ultimate use of the project (application) and the impact to the organization (impact).

Application/Impact Objectives Improve Facilitation

Objectives are the first information reviewed prior to facilitating a meeting or training session, and they define the facilitator's approach in teaching the project or program. They provide guidance for the facilitator to know how to present, what to present, and the context in which to present. More specifically, these higher levels of objectives provide facilitators with the information to:

- show the end result and provide the focus to achieve it
- focus the discussions on application and impact
- ensure that the participants have job-related experience
- teach to the test.

Application/Impact Objectives Help Participants Understand What Is Expected

Participants need clear direction as to why they are there and what they are expected to do. Essentially, the role of a participant changes with higher levels of objectives. Participants are expected to attend meetings and training, become involved and engaged, and to learn. By communicating application and impact objectives, participants will realize there is an expectation for them to apply what they learn and that the application of knowledge should reap results. Again, application and impact objectives remove the mystery from the program and the roles within it.

Impact Objectives Excite Sponsors

The sponsors (those who actually fund the program) often request data that shows how well the program achieved its goal. Impact measures resonate with executives and program sponsors. It is no secret that executives do not get excited about reaction and learning objectives. They are not as concerned with reactions to a program or even what is learned. Rather, their interest lies in what participants do with what they learn, and the ultimate impact it has on the organization. Impact objectives grab the attention of executives as they:

- connect the program to the business
- connect the program to key performance indicators (KPI)
- show the business value.

Application/Impact Objectives
Simplify Evaluation

These high-level objectives pave the way for evaluation by providing the focus and details needed for the evaluator to collect and analyze results. The primary reason, from an accountability perspective, to have higher levels of objectives is because they:

♦ identify data to be selected in the organization
♦ define specific measures reflected in the data
♦ suggest the appropriate data collection method
♦ suggest the source of data
♦ suggest the timing of data collection
♦ suggest responsibilities to collect data.

All Levels of Objectives Inform the Stakeholders

Collectively, all levels of evaluation help stakeholders understand the program more clearly and specifically. All stakeholders need to know not only why the program is being developed, but also about participant reaction, what the participants have learned, what actions they will take, and ultimately, what they will accomplish.

STEP **6**

Final Thoughts

This step presents information on how to set objectives with emphasis on higher levels: application, impact, and ROI. At business impact, the objectives provide the business alignment throughout the project. When present, business impact objectives keep the focus on business performance from all stakeholders. The step shows how to develop objectives at each of the five levels, recognizing that having impact objectives alone would not be sufficient. These objectives are sometimes missing from projects or programs, but they are absolutely essential. For more detail on developing objectives at multiple levels, please see the references.

Design for Results

OVERVIEW

The results expected from the program must be considered through all steps.

There are a variety of ways to communicate expectations, and the value of the participants in this project should not be overlooked.

Designing for results is related to designing for learning.

The seventh step focuses on designing the project or program to deliver results. Program design has an important connection to the results achieved. Designing for results throughout the life cycle ensures that the focus is always on results at every phase of the project, and that tools, templates, and processes are in place to ensure those results are achieved. This concept involves designing the appropriate communications about the program, changing the role of participants, and designing specific tools and content to make the project results-based.

STEP 7

Communicating with Results in Mind

When a program is implemented a chain of communications begins. These communications describe what is expected from the project, for all who are involved. The principal audience for communication is the individuals who will make the project successful; they are often labeled as the participants. The managers of these participants, who are expecting results in return for the participants' involvement in the project, are also a target for information. At least four areas of communication are important.

Announcements

Any announcement for the program—whether an announcement, online blurb, ad, email, or blog—should include expectations of results. No longer does the flyer focus on describing the program in terms of its content or learning objectives. The focus is now on what individuals will accomplish with a project and the business impact that it will deliver. The measure should be clearly articulated so it will answer the participant's first question, "What's in it for me?" This clearly captures the results-based philosophy of a particular program.

Brochures

If the project is ongoing or involves a significant number of participants, sometimes a brochure is developed. A brochure is typical for programs in learning and development, executive education, leadership development, process improvement, and major communication projects. These brochures are often cleverly written from a marketing perspective and are engaging and attractive. An added feature should be a description of the results that will be or have been achieved from the project, detailing specific outcomes at the application level (what individuals will accomplish) and the impact level, as well as the consequences of the application. For major conferences, for example, the brochure would typically have described the beautiful location, outstanding keynotes, effective learning environment, and the wonderful setting of the conference. Now, conference organizers describe what participants will achieve as a result of the conference. These additions can be powerful and make a tremendous difference on the outcome of the program.

Memos

Correspondence to participants before they become fully engaged with their program is critical. These memos and instructions should outline the results described in the announcements and brochures, and focus on what individuals should expect when they become involved in the project. When pre-work is necessary for participants to connect with the project, the focus should be on the results expected. Sometimes participants are asked to bring specific examples, case studies, problems, measures, or business challenges. Communications should be consistent with the results-based philosophy, underscore the expectations and requirements, and explain what must be achieved and accomplished. Also, the request to provide feedback and document results is explained to participants, emphasizing how they will benefit from responding.

Workbooks

Workbooks are designed with higher levels of objectives in mind. Application and impact objectives influence the design of exercises and activities as they emphasize results. Application tools are spaced throughout the workbook to encourage and facilitate action. Impact measures, and the context around them, appear in problems, case studies, learning checks, and skill practices.

STEP 7

Changing the Role of Participants

Perhaps there is no more important individual who can achieve business success than the participant involved in the program. For a formal learning and development program, the participant is the person who is learning the skill and knowledge needed for a job setting that will subsequently drive business performance if used properly. For other types of projects, the participant is the person who is involved in the implementation to achieve the results all the way through business impact. It is often the mindset of this person (e.g. the readiness and motivation of this individual to achieve success) that will make a difference. Sometimes this starts with changing the role of this person, defining more clearly what is expected and perhaps expanding expectations beyond what is traditionally required.

Why This Is Necessary

Many programs and projects fail because the individuals involved didn't do what they were supposed to do. While there are many barriers to achieving success, including those in the workplace, perhaps the most critical one is that the person involved did not want to, did not have time to, or did not see any reason to do what is necessary to achieve success. While they normally blame others (and not themselves), the participant may actually be the problem. The efforts of the participant must change, and this involves two issues, described next.

Defining the Role

The first issue is to define the role of the participant, clearly outlining what is expected. For formal learning and development, participants should always understand their specific roles. Table 7.1 describes the new and updated role of a participant in a formal learning and development program. This role clearly defines what is expected throughout the process and engages the participants in expectations beyond the formal sessions. It suggests that the success is not achieved until the consequence of application is obtained, identified as specific business improvements. Most importantly, the role requires participants to provide data. It is only through their efforts and subsequent information that others will understand their successes.

Documenting the Roles

The role of the participants should be clearly documented in several places. For formal learning and development, the role is sometimes

TABLE 7.1

The Role of the Participant

1. Be prepared to take advantage of the opportunity to learn, seeking value in any type of project or program.

2. Attend, be on time, stay fully engaged, and become a productive participant.

3. Look for the positives in the program and focus on how the impediments can be removed.

4. Meet or exceed the learning objectives, fully understanding what is expected.

5. Share experiences and expectations freely, recognizing that others are learning from you.

6. Plan to apply what is learned in a workplace setting.

7. Remove, minimize, or work around barriers to application and achieve success.

8. Apply the learning in a workplace setting, making adjustments and changes as necessary to be successful.

9. Follow through with the consequences of application, achieving the business results from the program.

10. When requested, provide data that shows your success as well as the barriers and enablers to success.

placed on the name tents so that it is clearly visible at all times during the workshop. In other cases, the role is presented as a handout in the beginning of the workshop, outlining what is expected of the participant all the way through to impact and results. Sometimes, it is included in the workbook material, usually as the first page. It is also placed in catalogs of programs where program descriptions are listed. The role can be included as an attachment to the registration documents as participants are enrolled in a program. It is often included in application documents, reminding the participant of his or her role. Finally, some learning centers place the roles in each conference room so they are clearly visible. The key issue in documenting roles is to place them permanently and prominently so that they are easily understood.

Creating Expectations

With the roles of participants clearly defined, expectations are created. The challenge is to let participants know what is expected and to avoid any surprises throughout the process. Participants resist surprises involving assignments, application tools, or action plans. Also, when a questionnaire, interview, or focus group is scheduled on a post-program basis, participants often resent these add-on activities. The approach is to position any necessary actions or data collection as a built-in process and not an add-on activity.

Identifying Measures before the Program

For some projects, the participants often define the specific business measures that need to improve. For example, in a leadership development program implemented in cross-functional areas, participants are often asked to identify the business measures that matter to them, but only if those measures can be changed working with their team using the competencies of the program. Although this approach may seem dysfunctional, it represents the ultimate customization for the participant, and it applies to many projects and programs. The implementation of lean Six Sigma, for example, requires participants to identify specific business measures that they want to improve by making a process more efficient or effective. Impact measures are identified and become part of the project undertaken by the participant. In the classic GE workout program, pioneered by GE's former chairman, Jack Welch, the participants identified specific projects that needed to improve. All types of process improvement and performance enhancement efforts have this opportunity ranging from negotiations, creativity, innovation, problem solving, communication, team building, coaching, leadership development, supervisor development, management development, and executive education, among others. This creates the expectation and often comes with a pleasant reaction, because the participant focuses on the measure that matters to them.

STEP 7

Involving the Managers

In addition to creating expectations directed to participants, the participants' managers may be involved. Participants may be asked to meet with their manager to ensure that the manager has input into the involvement in the program. Sometimes this includes an agreement about what must improve or change as a result of the program. One of the most powerful actions that can be taken is having the managers set goals with participants prior to the programs. More information on this later.

Messages from Executives

In addition to the immediate manager involvement, having others in executive roles to create expectations can be powerful. In most organizations, the top leaders are often highly respected, and their requirements or expectations are not only noticed, but are often influential. Figure 7.1 shows an opening announcement from a CEO about a safety project. This part of the opening speech clearly positions the expectations for business connections. When this speech was delivered to participants, it removed any doubt of what was expected. The message is clear: They must learn new approaches and tools that they will use or implement, but ultimately, success must be achieved at a business level.

Design for Learning

Almost every project involves learning. Of course, formal learning and development will usually include the acquisition of serious knowledge and skills. A prerequisite to designing for results is to make sure that the program is designed for proper learning. This involves several elements.

The Learning Style

Sometimes it is helpful to understand the learning style of the participants for particular age groups. For example, in a program for the Gen-Y generation, learning should be focused on technology. Older groups often need visual or participative approaches. Taking inventories on learning styles can help ensure that the project or program is matched with the preferred learning style of participants.

FIGURE 7.1
CEO Message and Expectations

CEO Message

Thank you for taking the time to become involved in this important project. I am confident that this is the right time and the right place to achieve some major safety improvements. Although we have a safety record that is among the best in the industry, there is still room for much improvement, and it is unacceptable in our minds and in your minds. There is no way we can be pleased with any lost time injuries, let alone a fatality in our workplace.

We have a dozen business measures that you are reviewing in this particular project. The focus of this project is to improve as many of these as possible. The measures will be ranked in the order of the seriousness in terms of pain and suffering for employees and also cost and disruption at the workplace. We expect you to make significant improvements in these measures.

During this project, you will be exposed to a variety of techniques and processes to achieve success. You have our support to make it a reality. Here is what a previous group of participants have achieved in this same project:

Measure	Reduction
Fatalities	50%
Lost time injuries	12%
Accident severity rate	12%
OSHA reportable injuries	13%
OSHA fines	18%
First aid treatments	23%
Near misses	16%
Property damage	29%
Down time because of accidents	18%

I think you can do even better than this amazing performance. I have confidence in you to accomplish this. You have my full support. You have the full support of our safety and health team. And you have the full support of your operating executives. There is nothing that we won't do to assist you in this effort. If you have a problem or issue that you need to get resolved and you are having difficulty, contact my office and I will take care of it.

The improvement in these measures is on your shoulders. Only you can do this. We cannot do it at a distance and our safety and health team cannot do it alone. It is your actions with your employees that can really make a difference.

Good luck and we look forward to celebrating these successes with you.

Sequencing and Timing

Sequencing the materials from easy to hard, or for the natural flow of the learning, is helpful. Advanced material is placed near the end. Small quantities of information should be presented sequentially, keeping a balance so not too much content is offered, but certainly enough to keep the individuals challenged.

The materials for learning should come at the right time for the participant, ideally, just before they need to use it. If it is presented too early, it will be forgotten; and if it is too late, they will have already learned another way to do it. Essentially, this challenge is to focus on achieving customized learning to the individual, following the J4 approach:

1. Just for me.
2. Just in time.
3. Just enough.
4. Just right for the task.

Design for Results

After designing for learning comes the focus on results. The two issues are connected. As the program is designed for participants

STEP
7

to learn the content, the focus shifts ultimately on the business results. At least five areas need attention.

Activities

All activities in the session should focus on situations that define the application of what participants are learning, the consequences of their learning, or both. Breakout sessions, working groups, individual projects, and any other assignments should focus on the actions that participants will be taking on the job to achieve business success.

Skill Practices

Sometimes participants will practice skills where the focus is on the use of those skills and the subsequent outcomes. The situational context for the practice is critical for achieving business results. For example, if a learning session is focused on improving employee work habits, a distinct set of skill sets are developed for changing these habits. To provide the focus, an impact objective is needed to define the original problem that must be changed. In one setting, it was absenteeism and tardiness. With that objective known, the skill practices are designed to improve an existing measure of unplanned absenteeism and persistent tardiness, both captured in the system. Without the impact objectives, the skill practice could be focusing on situations where other unrelated work habits and outcomes could be the problem, such as excessive talking, excessive texting, improper dress code, and other distracting habits. In this particular example, those outcomes were not the problem. The impact objectives clearly defined the problem and signaled for the designer to include absenteeism and tardiness in the skill practices.

Simulations

When simulations are developed to measure learning, they should describe and connect with the ultimate outcomes. This extra effort makes the simulation as real as possible for application and keeps an eye on the consequences (business impact). For example, simulations with the use of software are not only replicating what the participant is doing, but reporting time taken to accomplish steps (time), errors that are made along the way (quality), and level of accomplishment achieved (productivity). These simulations remind the individuals about the ultimate outcome, business results.

Problems

Some programs involve solving problems, particularly if the program is process oriented. The problems provided should reflect a realistic connection to application and impact. The problems' related activities should focus on a problem that participants will be solving and the measures that they will be improving as the problem is solved, such as output, quality, cost, and time. For example, in an advanced negotiation program, participants were asked to solve a negotiation problem. Given the ultimate outcome needed for the negations (budget, delivery, and quality), the participants used the appropriate skill sets to ultimately achieve their negotiations in a planned process. In solving the problem, participants had to identify the specific skill sets that would be used (application), and arrive at the correct amount for each outcome (business impact).

Case Studies

Case studies are often a part of programs, particularly for the learning and development field. Case studies bring to light real situations. Case studies should be selected that focus on the content, application, and impact for the program. Application items and impact measures should be scattered throughout the case study. The case study includes them, focuses on them, and often results in recommendations or changes to them. This reminds the audience of the ultimate impact that should be an important part of the process.

Built-In Application Tools

Building data collection tools into the project is perhaps one of the most important areas where designing for results works extremely well. This is particularly helpful for learning and development programs and other HR projects where data collection can easily be a part of the program. Ranging from simple action plans to significant job aids, the tools come in a variety of types and designs. They serve as application and data collection tools.

Action Plans

A simple process, the action plan is a tool that is completed during the program, outlining specifically what the participant will accomplish after the program is completed and during its implementation. The action plan always represents application data and can easily include business impact data where a business measure will be improved. Figure 7.2 shows an action plan where the focus is directly on improving a business measure. In this example, unplanned absenteeism in a call center is being improved from a high of 9% to a planned level of 5%. The actions listed in the plan on the left side of the document are the steps that will be taken to improve the business measure. The information on the right focuses more detail on the data including the value it delivers. While this tool serves as a data collection process, it keeps the focus on business impact. As the data are collected, it can even be used to isolate the effects of the program on the impact data, validating that the business alignment did occur. For this to work extremely well, several steps must be taken before, during, and after the action plan to keep the focus on business impact. Figure 7.3 shows the steps that are followed to ensure that the action plan is built into the process and becomes an integral part of achieving the business success.

Improvement Plans and Guides

Sometimes, the phrase "action plan" is not appropriate, as some organizations have used it to refer to many other projects and

FIGURE 7.2

Example of an Action Plan

Action Plan

Name: _Andy Nichols_ Facilitator Signature: _____ Follow-up date: _September 1_

Objective: _Reduce weekly absenteeism rate for team_

Evaluation Period: _March to April_

Improvement Measure: _Absenteeism rate_ Current Performance: _9%_ Target performance: _5%_

Action Steps		Analysis
1. Meet with team to discuss reasons for absenteeism—using problem solving skills.	10 March	A. What is the unit of measure? _One absence_
2. Review absenteeism records for each employee—look for trends and patterns.	20 March	B. What is the value (cost) of one unit? _$54.00_ C. How did you arrive at this value? _Standard value_
3. Counsel with "problem employees" to correct habits and explore opportunities for improvement.	20 March	D. How much did the measure change during the evaluation period? (monthly value) _3.5%_
4. Conduct a brief "performance discussion" with each employee returning to work after an unplanned absence.	20 March	E. What other factors could have contributed to this improvement? _Changes in job market and changes in disciplinary policy_
5. Provide recognition to employees who have perfect attendance.	20 March	F. What percent of this change was actually caused by this program? _40%_
6. Follow-up with each discussion and discuss improvement or lack of improvement and plan other action.	31 March	G. What level of confidence do you place on the above information? (100%= Certainty and 0%= No confidence) _80%_
7. Monitor improvement and provide recognition when appropriate.	31 March	
Intangible benefits: _Less stress, greater job satisfaction_		Comments: _Great program—it kept me on track with this problem_

STEP
7

FIGURE 7.3

Sequence of Activities for Action Planning

Before	• Communicate the action plan requirement early. • Require operating measures to be identified by participants.
During	• Describe the action planning process. • Allow time to develop the plan. • Teach the action planning process. • Have the facilitator approve the action plan. • Require participants to assign a monetary value for each proposed improvement (optional). • If possible, require action plans to be presented to the group. • Explain the follow-up mechanism.
After	• Require participants to provide improvement data. • Ask participants to isolate the effects of the program. • Ask participants to provide a level of confidence for estimates. • Collect action plans at the pre-determined follow up time. • Summarize the data and calculate the ROI (optional).

programs, sometimes leaving an unsavory image. When this is the case, other terms can be used. Some prefer the concept of improvement plans, recognizing that a business measure has been identified and improvement is needed. The improvement may represent the entire team or the improvement of an individual. There are many types of simple and effective designs for the process to work well. In addition to improvement plan, the term "application guide" can be used and can include a completed example as well as what is expected from the participant, including tips and techniques along the way to make it work.

Application Tools/Templates

Moving beyond action and improvement plans brings a variety of application tools such as simple forms to use, technology support to enhance an application, and guides to track and monitor business improvement. All types of templates and tools can be used to keep the process on track, provide data for those who need it, and remind a participant where he or she is going.

Performance Contract

Perhaps the most powerful built-in tool is the performance contract. This is essentially a contract for performance improvement between the participant in the project or program and his or her immediate manager. Before a program is conducted, the participant meets with the manager and they agree on the specific measures that should be improved and the amount of improvement. Essentially, they agree on an improvement that will result in the use of the content, information, and materials of the program. This contract can be enhanced if a third party enters the contractual arrangement (this would normally be the facilitator for the learning and development program or a project coordinator for other types of projects).

Performance contracts are powerful, as these individuals are now making a contract for performance change that will be achieved through the use of content and materials from the program, and has the added bonus of support from the immediate manager and from the facilitator/project manager. When programs are implemented using a performance contract they are powerful in delivering very significant changes in the business measure.

The design of the performance contract is similar to the action plan. Figure 7.4 shows a performance contract for a sales representative involved in a variety of sales enabling processes, including a combination of formal learning sessions, online tools, and coaching from the sales manager. The goal is to increase sales with existing clients. The sales manager approves the contract along with the participant and the facilitator of the project.

FIGURE 7.4

Example of a Performance Contract

Performance Contract

Name: Laura Gibson

Manager: Cathy Gettys

Facilitator: _____

Objective: Increase sales with existing clients by 20%

Evaluation Period: January to Marc

Improvement Measure: Monthly sales

Current Performance: $56,000 per month

Target performance: $67,000 per month

Action Steps		Analysis
Meet with key clients to discuss issues, concerns, and other opportunities.	31 January	What is the unit of measure? Monthly sales for existing clients
Review customer feedback data—look for trends and patterns.	1 February	What is the value (cost) of one unit? 25% profit margin
Counsel with "at risk" clients to correct problems and explore opportunities for improvement.	2 February	How did you arrive at this value? Standard value
Develop business plan for high-potential clients.	5 February	How much did the measure change during the evaluation period? (monthly value) $13,000
Provide recognition to clients with long tenure.	Routinely	What other factors could have contributed to this improvement? Changes in market, new promotion
Schedule appreciation dinner for key clients.	15 February	
Encourage marketing to delegate more responsibilities.	20 February	What percent of this change was actually caused by this program? 60%
Follow up with each discussion and discuss improvement and plan other action.	Routinely	
Monitor improvement and provide support when appropriate.	15 March	What level of confidence do you place on the above information? (100% = Certainty and 0% = No confidence) 90%
Intangible benefits: Client satisfaction, loyalty		Comments: Excellent, hard-hitting program

Job Aids

Job aids represent a variety of designs that help an individual achieve success with application and impact. The job aid illustrates the proper way of sequencing tasks and processes and reminds the individual what must be achieved, all with the ultimate aim of improving a business measure. Perhaps the simplest example is the job aid used at a major restaurant chain. The job aid shows what must go into a particular dish ordered by a customer. The individuals preparing the food use the job aid, which was part of a training program. The job aid shows how the process flows, using various photographs, arrows, charts, and diagrams. It is easily positioned at the station where the food is prepared and serves as a quick reference guide. When used properly, the job aid is driving important business measures: keeping the time to fill the order at a minimum (time savings), allowing the restaurant to serve more customers (productivity), and ensuring consistency with the meal and reducing the likelihood of a mistake being made on the order (quality).

Involving the Participant's Manager

A final area of design involves creating a role for the managers of the participants. As mentioned earlier, this is a very powerful group and having specific items, activities, tools, and templates for them can make a tremendous difference in business results.

The Most Influential Group

Research has consistently shown that the managers of a group of participants are the most influential group in helping participants achieve application and impact objectives, apart from their own motivation, desire, and determination. No other group can influence participants as much as their immediate managers. Figure 7.5 shows how learning is transferred to the job, using three important groups of stakeholders involved in this success: the participants, the immediate manager of the participants, and the facilitator. In a non-learning program, the facilitator is the project organizer. Three

FIGURE 7.5

The Transfer of Success to the Job

		Timeframe		
		Before	During	After
Roles	Manager	1	2	3
	Participant	4	5	6
	Facilitator/ Organizer	7	8	9

time frames are possible: prior to the program, during the program, and after the program.

This matrix creates nine possible blocks of activities to transfer what is learned from a particular program to the job. The transfer not only includes the behaviors and actions that must be taken (application), but also the impact that must be obtained (impact measures). For example, the participant can be involved in pre-project activities to set specific goals that he or she wants to achieve before the project is implemented (block number 4). During the program, the participant will plan specific actions to improve a business measure (block number 5). After the program is conducted, the participant will apply the material, achieve the business impact improvement, and report it to interested stakeholders (block number 6).

In another example, the manager can meet with the participant and set a goal before attending the program (block number 1). During the implementation, the manager observes part of the program, teaches a segment of it, or provides coaching as part of it (block number 2). After the program is conducted, the manager follows up to make sure that the material is used appropriately and the business impact has been achieved (block number 3). The process continues until activities are identified for every block.

Research on this matrix shows that the most powerful blocks for achieving learning transfer to the job are blocks 1 and 3. Unfortunately, managers do not always see it that way. They underestimate their influence. They must be reminded of their influence and provided tools that take very little time to apply to ensure the result of the project is used and drives the business results. This is one of the most powerful areas to explore for improving business results.

Pre-Project Activities

At the very least, managers should set expectations for participants involved in any type of activity, program, project, event, or initiative. It only takes a matter of minutes to set that expectation and the results can be powerful. Pre-project activities can range from a formal process of a performance contract, described earlier, to an informal, two-minute discussion that takes place prior to being involved in the program. A full array of activities should be provided that take very little time. Even a script could be helpful. The important point is that these managers must be reminded, encouraged, or even required to do this.

During the Project Activities

Sometimes, it is important for the manager to have input into the design and development of the program. Possible activities include having managers (or at least someone representing the manager group) help in designing the content of the program. Also, managers could review the content and serve as subject experts to approve it. Managers could be involved in the program, teaching parts of the process, providing one-on-one coaching for participants needing help with specific parts, or just observing the program (or a portion of it). Managers could serve on an advisory committee for the program or review the success of others in the program. The key is to connect the manager to the design and content of the program. Manager involvement will help focus the program on business results, which they will find extremely important.

Post-Project Activities

The most basic action a manager can take is to follow up to ensure the content of the project is being used properly. Suggesting, encouraging, or even requiring application and impact can be very powerful. Managers should be available to provide assistance and support as needed to make the program successful. Just being available as a sounding board or to run interference to ease the application may be enough. Although not necessary, post-project activities can be more involved on a formal basis, where the managers actively participate in follow-up evaluations. Managers may sign off on results, review a questionnaire, follow up on action plans, collect data, or present the results. In any case, they make a difference.

Reinforcement Tools

In some situations, a management reinforcement workshop is offered to teach managers how to reinforce and guide the behaviors needed to achieve a desired level of performance in business measures. Reinforcement workshops are very brief, usually ranging from two hours to half a day, but can be extremely valuable. Some formal learning programs come with management reinforcement or management support workshops. In addition to the workshops, a variety of tools can be created and sent to managers. The tools include checklists, scripts, key questions, resources, and contacts needed to keep the focus on results.

Sometimes managers volunteer for a coaching role where they are asked to be available to assist the participants with a formal coaching process. In this scenario, managers are provided details about coaching, how to make it work, and what is required of them. In more formal programs they will actually receive some coaching training. This training is extremely powerful when a participant's immediate manager serves as a coach to accomplish business results.

Final Thoughts

This step focuses on what is necessary to achieve business results from a design perspective—designing the communications, expectations, roles, content, and tools that are necessary for a participant to be fully involved. A program with the proper design, combined with a participant who is motivated to learn, will make achieving success a reality. Participants will explore connections to use the acquired knowledge and increase the tenacity to implement the tools and techniques. This approach provides the readiness, motivation, commitment, and tools needed to help achieve business alignment. The next step focuses on collecting the impact data.

STEP **7**

Measure the Business Impact

OVERVIEW

Specific impact measures, linked to specific programs, must be monitored. All possibilities for monitoring must be considered in order to accurately measure the business impact of a program.

Monitoring performance data enables management to track performance.

When certain data are not readily available and data collection becomes time consuming and expensive, there are alternatives in data collection methods.

The eighth step focuses on tracking business performance measures. Most sponsors regard business impact data as the most important data type because of its connection to the success of the organization. This is the first step in a two part process to validate the business alignment. This chapter covers the specific processes needed to collect business measures after the program is implemented. Coverage includes monitoring the record-keeping systems, implementing action plans, and using questionnaires. These three processes account for most opportunities available for collecting business impact data.

STEP 8

Specific Measures Linked to Programs

An important issue that often surfaces when considering business alignment is the understanding of specific measures that are often driven by specific programs. While there are no standard answers, Table 8.1 represents a summary of some typical business measures for specific types of programs. The measures are quite broad for some programs. For example, leadership development may pay off

TABLE 8.1

Typical Impact Measures for Projects and Programs

Program	Key Impact Measurements
Absenteeism control/ reduction	Absenteeism, customer satisfaction, delays, job satisfaction, productivity, stress
Association meetings	Costs, customer service, job satisfaction, productivity, quality, sales, time, turnover
Business coaching	Costs, customer satisfaction, efficiency, employee satisfaction, productivity/output, quality, time savings
Career development/ career management	Job satisfaction, promotions, recruiting expenses, turnover
Communications programs	Conflicts, errors, job satisfaction, productivity, stress
Compensation plans	Costs, job satisfaction, productivity, quality
Compliance programs	Charges, losses, penalties/fines, settlements
Diversity	Absenteeism, charges, complaints, losses, settlements, turnover
Employee retention programs	Engagement, job satisfaction, promotions, turnover
Engineering/technical conferences	Costs, customer satisfaction, cycle times, downtime, job, satisfaction, process time, productivity/output, quality, waste
Ethics programs	Fines, fraud, incidents, penalties, theft
E-Learning	Cost savings, cycle times, error reductions, job satisfaction, productivity improvement, quality improvement
Executive education	Absenteeism, costs, customer service, job satisfaction, productivity, quality, sales, time, turnover
Franchise/dealer meetings	Cost of sales, customer loyalty, market share, quality, efficiency, sales
Golfing events	Customer loyalty, market share, new accounts, sales, upselling
Labor-management cooperation programs	Absenteeism, grievances, job satisfaction, work stoppages
Leadership	Cost/time savings, development, efficiency, employee satisfaction, engagement, productivity/output, quality

Management development	Absenteeism, costs, customer service, job satisfaction, productivity, quality, sales, time, turnover
Marketing programs	Brand awareness, churn rate, cross-selling, customer loyalty, customer satisfaction, market share, new acounts, sales, upselling
Medical meetings	Compliance, efficiency, medical costs, patient satisfaction, quality
Orientation, onboarding	Early turnover, performance, productivity, quality of work, training time
Personal productivity/ time management	Job satisfaction, productivity, stress reduction, time savings
Project management	Budgets, quality improvement, time savings
Quality programs	Costs, cycle times, defects, response times, rework
Retention management	Engagement, job satisfaction, turnover
Safety programs	Accident frequency rates, accident severity rates, first aid treatments
Sales meetings	Customer loyalty, market share, new accounts, sales
Self-directed teams	Absenteeism, customer satisfaction, job satisfaction productivity/output, quality, turnover
Sexual harassment prevention	Absenteeism, complaints, employee satisfaction, turnover
Six Sigma/lean projects	Costs, cycle times, defects, response times, rework, waste
Software projects	Absenteeism, costs, customer service, job satisfaction, productivity, quality, sales, time, turnover
Stress management	Absenteeism, job satisfaction, medical costs, turnover
Supervisor/team leader programs	Absenteeism, complaints, costs, job satisfaction, productivity, quality, sales, time, turnover
Team-building	Absenteeism, costs, customer service, job satisfaction, productivity, quality, sales, time, turnover
Wellness/fitness programs	Absenteeism, accidents, medical costs, turnover

STEP 8

in a variety of measures, such as improved productivity, enhanced sales and revenues, improved quality, cycle-time reduction, direct cost savings, and employee job satisfaction. In other programs, the influenced measures are quite narrow. For example, labor-management cooperation programs typically influence grievances, work stoppages, and employee satisfaction. Orientation programs typically influence measures of early turnover (turnover in the first ninety days of employment), initial job performance, and productivity. The measures that are influenced depend on the objectives and the design of the program. The table also illustrates the immense number of measures that can be driven or influenced.

A word of caution is needed. Presenting specific measures linked to a typical program may give the impression that these are the only measures influenced. In practice, a program can have many outcomes. Table 8.1 shows the most likely measures that arise from the studies that the ROI Institute has reviewed. In the course of a decade, we have been involved in over 2,000 studies, and common threads exist among particular programs.

The good news is that most programs are driving business measures. The measures are based on what is being changed in the various business units, divisions, regions, and individual workplaces. These are the measures that matter to senior executives. The difficulty often comes in ensuring that the connection to the program exists. This is accomplished through a variety of techniques to isolate the effects of the program on the particular business measures and will be discussed in the next chapter.

Business Performance Monitoring

Data are available in every organization to measure business performance. Monitoring performance data enables management to measure performance in terms of output, quality, costs, time, job satisfaction, and customer satisfaction, among other measures. In determining the source of data in the evaluation, the first consideration should be existing databases, reports, and scorecards.

In most organizations, performance data suitable for measuring program-related improvement are available. If not, additional record-keeping systems will have to be developed for measurement and analysis. At this point, the question of economics surfaces. Is it economical to develop the record-keeping systems necessary to evaluate a program? If the costs are greater than the expected benefits, developing those systems is pointless.

Identify Appropriate Measures

Existing performance measures should be thoroughly researched to identify those related to the proposed objectives of the program. Often, several performance measures are related to the same item. For example, the efficiency of a production unit can be measured in several ways:

- the number of units produced per hour
- the number of on-schedule production units
- the percentage of equipment used
- the percentage of equipment downtime
- the labor cost per unit of production
- the overtime required per unit of production
- total unit cost.

Each of these, in its own way, measures the effectiveness or efficiency of the production unit. All related measures should be reviewed to determine those most relevant to the program.

Convert Current Measures to Usable Ones

Occasionally, existing performance measures are integrated with other data, and keeping them isolated from unrelated data may be difficult. In this situation, all existing, related measures should be extracted and tabulated again to make them more appropriate for comparison in the evaluation. At times, conversion factors may be necessary. For example, the average number of new sales orders per month may be presented regularly in the performance measures for the sales department. In addition, the sales costs per sales

STEP 8

representative are also presented. However, in the evaluation of a program, the average cost per new sale is needed. The average number of new sales orders and the sales cost per sales representative are required to develop the data necessary for comparison.

The Use of Action Plans to Collect Business Impact Data

For many projects and programs, business data are readily available. However, at times, data won't be easily accessible to the evaluator. Sometimes, data are maintained at the individual, work unit, or department level and may not be known to anyone outside that area. Tracking down those data sets may be too expensive and time-consuming. When this is the case, other data collection methods may be used to capture data sets and make them available for the evaluator. Three other options are described in this book: the use of action plans, performance contracts, and questionnaires. Action plans and performance contracts were briefly discussed in Step 7. This section provides more detail.

Action plans can be a useful tool for capturing business impact data. For business impact data, the action plan is more focused and credible than a questionnaire. The following steps are recommended when an action plan is developed and implemented to capture business impact data and to convert the data to monetary values.

Set Goals and Targets

As shown in Figure 8.1, an action plan can be developed with a direct focus on business impact data. The plan presented in this figure requires participants to develop an overall objective for the plan, which is usually the primary objective of the program. In some cases, a program may have more than one objective, which requires additional action plans. In addition to the objective, the improvement measure and the current levels of performance are identified. This information requires that the participant anticipate the application of skills and set goals for specific performances that can be realized.

The action plan is completed during the program, often with input and assistance from the facilitator. The facilitator actually approves the plan, indicating that it meets the requirements of

FIGURE 8.1

Using the Action Plan Process

Name: _____
Objective: _____
Improvement Measure: _____

Facilitator Signature: _____
Evaluation Period _____ to _____
Current Performance: _____

Follow-Up Date: _____
Target Performance: _____

Action Steps	Analysis
1. _____	A. What is the unit of measure? _____
2. _____	B. What is the value (cost) of one unit? $ _____
3. _____	C. How did you arrive at this value? _____
4. _____	D. How much did the measure change during the evaluation period? (monthly value) _____
5. _____	E. List the other factors that have influenced this change. _____
6. _____	F. What percent of this change was actually caused by this program? _____ %
7. _____	G. What level of confidence do you place on the above information? (100%=Certainty and 0%=No Confidence) _____ %
Intangible benefits: _____	Comments: _____

being specific, motivating, achievable, realistic, and time-based (SMART). The plan can actually be developed in a one- to two-hour timeframe and often begins with action steps related to the program. These action steps are Level 3 activities that detail application and implementation. All these steps build support for, and are linked to, business impact measures.

Define the Unit of Measure

The next important step is to define the actual unit of measure. In some cases, more than one measure may be used and will subsequently be contained in additional action plans. The unit of measure is necessary to break the process into the simplest steps so that its ultimate value can be determined. Examples are: one unit manufactured, one package delivered, one percent increase in market share, one reject, one error, one defect, one grievance, one complaint, one absence, or one less person on welfare. The point is to break down impact data into the simplest terms possible.

Place a Monetary Value on Each Improvement

As an optional step, participants are asked to locate, calculate, or estimate the monetary value for each improvement outlined in their plans. The unit value is determined using a variety of methods such as standard values, expert input, external databases, or estimates. In the worst-case scenario, participants are asked to calculate the value. The process used in arriving at the value is described in the instructions for the action plan. When the actual improvement occurs, participants will use these values to capture the annual monetary benefits of the plan. This step is absolutely necessary for calculating the ROI for the program.

Implement the Action Plan

Participants implement the action plan after the program is conducted. The participants follow action plan steps, and the subsequent business impact results are achieved.

Provide Specific Improvements

At the end of the specified follow-up period—e.g., three months, six months, nine months, or one year—the participants indicate the specific improvements made, usually expressed as a daily, weekly, or monthly amount. This determines the actual amount of change that has been observed, measured, or recorded.

Isolate the Effects of the Program

Although the action plan is initiated because of the program, the actual improvements reported on the action plan may be influenced by other factors. Therefore, the program should not be given full credit for all of the improvement. While several methods are available for isolating the effects of a program, participant estimation is usually most appropriate in the action planning process. Participants are asked to estimate the percentage of the improvement directly related to the program.

Provide a Confidence Level for Estimates

The process to isolate the amount of the improvement directly related to the program is not precise. Participants are asked to indicate their level of confidence in their estimates. Using a scale of 0 to 100 percent—where 0 percent means no confidence and 100 percent means the estimates represent absolute certainty—participants have a way to express their confidence in the estimates.

Collect Action Plans at Specified Time Intervals

An excellent response rate is essential, so several steps may be necessary to ensure that the action plans are completed and returned. Usually, participants will see the importance of the process and will develop their plans during the program. Some organizations use follow-up reminders by mail or email. Others call participants to check progress. Still others offer assistance in developing the final plan. These steps may require additional resources, which must be weighed against the importance of having more precise data.

STEP 8

Summarize the Data

If developed properly, each action plan should have annualized monetary values associated with improvements. Also, each individual should have indicated the percentage of the improvement directly related to the program. Finally, participants should have provided a confidence percentage to reflect their certainty with the estimates and the subjective nature of some of the data that they provided.

Advantages of Action Plans

The action-planning process has several inherent advantages as a useful way to collect business impact data. Most of the data are taken directly from participants and often have the credibility needed for the analysis. Also, much of the responsibility for the analysis and evaluation is shifted to the participants as they address three of the most critical parts of the process.

Use of Performance Contracts to Measure Business Impact

The performance contract is a variation of the action plan. Based on the principle of mutual goal setting, a performance contract is a written agreement between a participant and the participant's manager. The participant agrees to improve performance in an area of concern related to the program. The agreement is in the form of a goal to be accomplished during the program or after program completion. The agreement details what is to be accomplished, at what time, and with what results.

Although the steps can vary according to the organization and the specific contract, a common sequence of events follows:

1. The employee (participant) becomes involved in the program implementation.

2. The participant and immediate manager mutually agree on a measure or measures for improvement related to the program (What's in it for me?).
3. Specific, measurable goals for improvement are set, following the SMART requirements.
4. In the early stages of the program, the contract is discussed, and plans are developed to accomplish the goals.
5. During program implementation, the participant works on the contract against a specific deadline.
6. The participant reports the results of the effort to the manager.
7. The manager and participant document the results and forward a copy to the program team along with appropriate comments.

The process of selecting the area for improvement is similar to the process used when preparing an action plan.

The Use of Questionnaires to Collect Business Impact Data

Using questionnaires for impact data collection brings both good news and bad news. The good news is that questionnaires are easy to implement and low-cost. Data analysis is very efficient, and the time to provide the data is often short, making them among the least disruptive data collection methods. However, the bad news is that the data can be distorted, inaccurate, and sometimes missing. The challenge is to take all the steps necessary to ensure that questionnaires are complete, accurate, clear, and returned on time.

Unfortunately, because of the disadvantages, questionnaires represent the weakest method of data collection. Paradoxically, they are the most often used method because of their advantages. For example, of the first 100 case studies published on the ROI methodology, roughly 50 percent used questionnaires for data collection. They are popular because they are convenient, low-cost, and fortunately or unfortunately, a way of life. The challenge is to make questionnaires credible and useful by ensuring that they capture all the necessary data, participants provide accurate and complete data, and the return rates are in the 70- to 80-percent range.

In the worst-case situation, the evaluator doesn't have a clue which measures have been driven or influenced by the program. For some, this situation may be inconceivable, but in practice it occurs routinely. Consider the tremendous sums of money poured into executive education, management development, leadership development, and executive coaching. Much of that, if not the vast majority, is implemented without any clue as to how those programs will add value, let alone improve some specific measure that might be connected to the program. When this is the case, the data collection instrument should follow the series of questions shown in Figure 8.2. This is much like a fishing expedition, as the evaluator attempts to uncover a particular business measure connected to the program. Still, it could be a useful exercise with some surprising results.

Question 1 is an attempt to connect the program to the work environment—it's the transition. It is essentially a Level 3 question about application, getting the participant to reflect on what actions they have taken because of the program. Question 2 examines consequences, defining or explaining more specifically the outcomes of their actions, implementation, and behaviors. The influence could be with individual work, the team, or even the organization. Question 3 asks for the specifics, defining the measure. In some cases, if not most, more than one measure may be involved, and these questions can have multiple responses. Question 4 is the actual unit value, which is profit if it is a sales-related output measure, or costs if it is a quality or time measure. This is a difficult challenge, but it is doable in some organizations because the unit values are already developed. Question 5 gauges the credibility of the data provided in Question 4. The participant explains how he or she arrived at the unit value. If Question 5 is left blank, the data item is thrown out (but the participants know this from the instructions). In essence, this would be an unsupported claim that is omitted from the analysis.

STEP **8**

FIGURE 8.2

Chain of Impact Questions When the Measure Is Unknown

1. How did you use the material from this program?

2. What influence did it have in your work? Team?

3. What specific measure was influenced? Define it.

4. What is the unit value of the measure? (Profit or Cost)

5. What is the basis of this value?

6. How much did the measure change since the program was conducted?

7. What is the frequency of the measure? Daily, weekly, monthly, etc.

8. What is the total annual value of the improvement?

9. List the other factors that could have caused this total improvement.

10. What percent of the total improvement can be attributed to this program?

11. What is your confidence estimate, expressed as a percent, for the above data? 0% = no confidence; 100% = certainty

Question 6 documents the change, the pre- and post-differences for the specific measure. Question 7 details the specific frequency, such as daily, weekly, or monthly data. The frequency is necessary to calculate the total annual improvement, asked for in Question 8. This is the first-year value of improvement. Most programs will only pay off on the first year of value, although long-term programs will have a longer period. Question 9 requires that participants think through other factors that might have influenced the specific measure that they reported. This is a way of validating the reported change. Initially, the participant may think that the improvement is all directly connected to this program. In reality, other factors are there, and this question provides an opportunity for participants to reflect on the links to other factors.

Question 10 then asks the participants to decide, after thinking about other possible factors, what percentage of the improvement came directly from the program, isolating the effects of the program from other influences. Because this is an estimate, it is adjusted for error, and asked for in Question 11.

Participants should not be surprised by these questions. They must know that they are coming, and every effort must be taken to get them to respond. Still, many professionals may consider this series of questions a futile exercise—that participants cannot provide responses. Fortunately, the research does not support this position. In literally hundreds of studies where this kind of approach is taken, participants can and will provide data connected to the program, assuming of course, that a connection to a business measure exists.

The skeptics often consider participants to be unknowing, uncooperative, and irresponsible, validating their point that the data would not be forthcoming. However, participants will provide data for four basic reasons:

1. They are the most credible source, since they are directly involved and understand the full scope of the program and its consequences.
2. It's their work, and they know more about it than anyone. Their performance is being reported and analyzed.
3. This process recognizes their roles as experts. The fact that this questionnaire is offered suggests that they are in a position to know, and they appreciate the recognition that they have the expertise to provide the data.
4. They are responsible. For the most part, participants will provide data if they understand why data are needed and how it will be used. Of course, not every participant will warm up to this exercise. It works extremely well for professional, engineering, administrative, management, and technical personnel. Operators, laborers, and entry-level clerical staff may have more difficulty. But in most situations, the participants are responsible and knowledgeable

and care about the process. Because of this, the quality and quantity of the data may be surprising.

Final Thoughts

The good news is that business impact data are readily available and very credible. This step provides an overview of several data collection approaches that can be used to capture business data. Many options are available. Some methods are gaining acceptance for use in business impact analysis. In addition to performance monitoring, follow-up questionnaires, action plans, and performance contracts are used regularly to collect data for impact analysis. The credibility of data will always be an issue when this level of data is collected and analyzed. Several strategies are offered to enhance the credibility of data analysis. The next step focuses on isolating the impact of the program on the data.

STEP 8

Isolate the Effects of the Program

OVERVIEW

In order to accurately determine the effects of a program on the business measures, all influences and other factors must be identified.

A variety of techniques can be implemented in order to isolate the effects of a program.

The ninth step focuses on separating the influence of the program from other influences. In almost every program, multiple influences drive the business measures. With multiple influences, measuring the effect of each one is important, or at least the portion attributed to the program. Without this isolation, program success will be in question. The results will be inappropriate and overstated if it is suggested that all the change in the business impact measure is attributed to the program. When this issue is ignored, the impact study is considered invalid and inconclusive.

Identifying Other Factors: A First Step

As a first step in isolating a program's impact on performance, all key factors that may have contributed to the performance improvement should be identified. This step communicates to interested parties that other factors may have influenced the results, underscoring that the program is not the sole source of improvement. Consequently, the credit for improvement is shared with several

STEP 9

possible variables and factors—an approach that is likely to gain the respect of the client.

Several potential sources are available to identify influencing variables. If the program is implemented on the request of a sponsor, then the sponsor may identify other initiatives or factors that might influence the output variable. Participants are usually aware of other influences that may have caused performance improvement. After all, the impacts of their collective efforts are being monitored and measured. In many situations, they have witnessed previous movements in the performance measures and can pinpoint reasons for changes.

The program implementation team is another source for identifying variables that impact results. Although the needs analysis will sometimes uncover these influencing variables, designers, developers, and facilitators may be able to identify the other factors while implementing the program.

In some situations, the immediate managers of participants may be able to identify variables that influence the business impact measure. This is particularly useful when participants are non-exempt employees (operatives) who may not be fully aware of the other variables that can influence performance.

Subject matter experts (SMEs) may identify other factors. These are the experts involved in the content of the program. They often analyze the need for the program, help design a specific solution, or provide specifications for implementation. They are knowledgeable about these issues, and their expertise may be helpful in identifying the other factors that could affect the program.

Other process owners may be able to provide input. For most situations, other processes are adding value. Could it be technology, restructuring, job design, new processes, quality initiatives, re-engineering, transformation, or change management? These are all likely processes inside an organization, and the owners of these processes will know whether their processes are in place or have been implemented during this same time period.

Finally, in the area in which the program is implemented, middle and top management may be able to identify other influences. Perhaps they have monitored, examined, and analyzed the variables previously. The authority of these individuals often increases the data's credibility.

Taking the time to focus attention on factors and variables that may have influenced performance brings additional accuracy and credibility to the process. It moves beyond presenting results with no mention of other influences—an approach that often destroys credibility. It also provides a foundation for some of the techniques described in this book by identifying the variables that must be isolated to show the effects of a program.

Using Control Groups

The most accurate approach for isolating the impact of a program is the use of control groups in an experimental design process. This approach involves the comparison of an experimental group involved in the program and a control group that is not. The composition of both groups should be as identical as possible and, if feasible, participants for each group should be selected randomly. When this is achieved and both groups are subjected to the same environmental influences, the difference in the performance of the two groups can be attributed to the program as illustrated in Figure 9.1.

For example, in a sales training program for Dell Computer Corporation, a control group arrangement was used. The program involved regional sales managers, account managers, account executives, account representatives, and sales representatives. The output measures were profit-margin quota attainment, total revenue attainment, profit margin, and various sales volumes. An experimental group was involved in the program and was carefully matched with a control group that was not involved. The equivalent number of participants for the control group was selected at random using the company database. To ensure that the control

FIGURE 9.1

Use of Control Groups

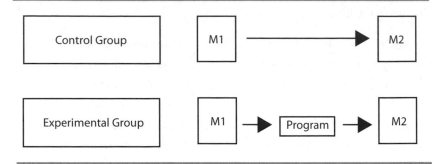

group and the program group were equivalent, selections were made on three criteria: job positions, job levels, and experience.

The control group and experimental groups do not necessarily have pre-program measurements. Measurements can be taken during the program and after the program is implemented, and the difference in the performance of the two groups shows the amount of improvement that is directly related to the program.

One concern with the use of control groups is that they may create an image of a laboratory setting, which can make some executives and administrators uncomfortable. To avoid this stigma, some organizations conduct a pilot program using participants as the experimental group. A similarly matched, non-participating control group is selected but does not receive any communication about the program. The terms "pilot program" and "comparison group" are a little less threatening than "experimental group" and "control group."

The control group approach does have some inherent problems that may make it difficult to apply in practice. The first problem is the selection of the groups. From a theoretical perspective, having identical control and experimental groups is next to impossible. Dozens of factors can affect performance, some of them individual, others contextual. To address this problem on a practical basis, it

STEP
9

is best to select four to six variables that will have the greatest influence on performance, using the concept of the 80/20 rule, or Pareto principle. With the 80/20 rule, the factors that might account for 80 percent of the difference and the most important factors are used.

Another problem with control groups is that the process is not appropriate for all situations. For some programs and processes, withholding the program from one group while it is implemented in another may not be appropriate. This is particularly important for critical solutions that are needed immediately. This barrier keeps many control groups from being implemented. Management is not willing to withhold a solution in one area to see how it works in another.

In practice, however, many opportunities arise for a possibility of a natural control group arrangement. If it will take several months for everyone in the organization to be involved in the solution, there may be enough time for a parallel comparison between the initial group and the last group. In these cases, ensuring that the groups are matched as closely as possible is critical so that the first group is similar to the last. These naturally occurring control groups often exist in major enterprise-wide program implementations. The challenge is to address this issue early enough to influence the implementation schedule so that similar groups can be used in the comparison.

Another problem is contamination, which can develop when participants involved in the program group (experimental group) actually communicate with others who are in the control group. Sometimes, the reverse situation occurs when members of the control group model the behavior of the experimental group. In either case, the experiment becomes contaminated as the influence of the program is passed to the control group. This can be minimized by ensuring that control groups and program groups are at different locations, have different shifts, or are on different floors in the same building. When this is not possible, explain to both groups that one group will be involved in the program now and the other

STEP 9

will be involved at a later date. Also, appealing to the sense of responsibility of those involved in the program and asking them not to share the information with others might be helpful.

Closely related to the previous problem is the issue of time. The longer a control group and experimental group comparison operates, the more likely other influences will affect the results. More variables will enter into the situation, contaminating the results. On the other end of the scale, there must be enough time so that a clear pattern can emerge between the two groups. Therefore, the timing for control group comparisons must strike a delicate balance of waiting long enough for their performance differences to show, but not so long that the results become seriously contaminated.

Another problem occurs when the different groups function under different environmental influences. This is usually the case when groups are at different locations. Sometimes, the selection of the groups can help prevent this problem. Another tactic is to use more groups than necessary and discard those with environmental differences.

Because the use of control groups is an effective approach for isolating impact, it should be considered as a technique when a business alignment is planned. In these situations, isolating the program impact with a high level of accuracy is important, and the primary advantage of the control group process is accuracy.

Using Trend-Line Analysis

Another useful technique for approximating the impact of a program is trend-line analysis. With this approach, a trend line is drawn to project the future, using previous performance as a base. After the program is conducted, actual performance is compared to the trend-line projection. Any improvement of performance over what the trend line predicted can then be reasonably attributed to program implementation. While this is not an exact process, it provides a reasonable estimation of the program's impact.

FIGURE 9.2

Trend-Line Analysis

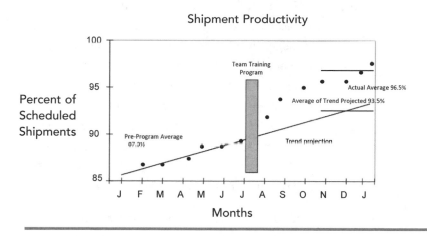

Shipment Productivity

Percent of Scheduled Shipments

Team Training Program

Actual Average 96.5%

Average of Trend Projected 93.5%

Pre-Program Average 87.3%

Trend projection

Months

Figure 9.2 shows an example of a trend-line analysis taken from a shipping department of a book distribution company. The percentage reflects the level of actual shipments compared to scheduled shipments. Data are presented before and after program implementation in July. As shown in the figure, an upward trend on the data began prior to program implementation. Although the program apparently had an effect on shipment productivity, the trend line shows that some improvement would have occurred anyway, based on the trend that had previously been established. Program leaders may have been tempted to measure the improvement by comparing the average six months' shipments prior to the program (87.3 percent) to the average six months after the program (96.5 percent), yielding a 9.2 percent difference. However, a more accurate comparison is the six-month average after the program compared to the trend line (93.5 percent). In this analysis, the difference is 3 percent. Using this more conservative measure increases the accuracy and credibility of the analysis.

To use this technique, two conditions must be met:

1. The trend that has developed prior to the program is expected to continue if the program had not been conducted.

Thus, the question posed is: Would this trend continue on the same path established before the participants attended the program? The process owner(s) should be able to provide input to reach this conclusion. If the answer is "no," the trend-line analysis will not be used. If the answer is "yes," the second condition is considered.

2. No new variables or influences entered the process during the evaluation period. The key word is "new," realizing that the trend has been established because of the influences already in place, yet no additional influences enter the process beyond conducting the program. If the answer is "yes," another method would have to be used. If the answer is "no," the trend-line analysis develops a reasonable estimate of the impact of this program.

Pre-program data must be available before this technique can be used, and the data should have some reasonable degree of stability. If the variance of the data is high, the stability of the trend line becomes an issue. If this is an extremely critical issue and the stability cannot be assessed from a direct plot of the data, more detailed statistical analyses can be used to determine whether the data are stable enough to make the projection. The trend line can be projected directly from historical data using a simple routine that is available with many calculators and software packages, such as Microsoft Excel.

Forecasting

A more analytical approach to trend-line analysis is the use of forecasting methods that predict a change in performance variables. This approach represents a mathematical interpretation of the trend-line analysis when other variables enter a situation during the evaluation period. With this approach, the output measure targeted by the program is forecast based on the influence of other variables that have changed during the evaluation period. The actual value of the measure is compared to the forecasted value. The difference reflects the contribution of the program.

With the forecasting approach, a major disadvantage occurs when several variables enter the process. The complexity multiplies, and the use of sophisticated statistical packages for multiple variable analyses is necessary. Even then, a good fit of the data to the model may not be possible. Unfortunately, some organizations have not developed mathematical relationships for output variables as a function of one or more inputs, and without them, the forecasting method is difficult to use.

The primary advantage of this process is that it can accurately predict business performance measures without the program, if appropriate data and models are available.

Estimates

Unfortunately, the most common method of isolating the effects of a program is the use of estimates from individuals. Estimating the amount of improvement connected to a particular program is the least effective method from an analytical viewpoint and, because it is the weakest method, every step should be taken to make it as credible as possible. The good news is that this can be a very credible process if some precautions are taken, as described in this section.

The beginning point in using this method is ensuring that the isolation is performed by the most credible source, and that is often not a higher-level manager or an executive removed from the process. The individual who provides this information must be able to understand how the program affects the impact measures. Essentially, there are four categories of input. Often, the most credible are the participants directly involved in the program and the managers of the participants, if they are close to the situation. Customers give credible estimates in unique situations where they are involved. External experts may also be very helpful. These are all described in this section.

Participants' Estimate of Impact

An easily implemented method for isolating the impact of a program is to obtain information directly from participants (users) during program implementation. The effectiveness of this approach rests on the assumption that participants are capable of determining or estimating how much of a performance improvement is related to the program implementation. Because their actions have produced the improvement, participants may have highly accurate input on the issue. They should know how much of the change was caused by implementing the program solution. Although an estimate, this value will usually have considerable credibility with management because they know participants are at the center of the change or improvement. Participant estimation is obtained by asking participants a series of questions:

◆ What other factors have contributed to this improvement in performance?

◆ What is the link between these factors and the improvement?

◆ What percentage of this improvement can be attributed to the implementation of this program?

◆ What confidence do you have in this estimate, expressed as a percentage? (0 percent = no confidence; 100 percent = complete confidence)

◆ What other individuals or groups could estimate this percentage to determine the amount attributed to this program?

An example will help describe the situation. In an effort to increase recycling in the community, three actions were taken. Recycling had been available but because of the apathy of the community, the inconvenience of the location, and a lack of incentive to do it—the results were not acceptable. The community implemented three new approaches. One approach was to conduct awareness sessions in the schools, neighborhoods, community groups, and churches to make people aware of recycling and what it means to them and the environment. In addition, the process of recycling was made more convenient; residents could place three different containers on the street and have them picked up. Additionally, if the citizens participated in recycling, a discount would be provided to their regular waste management bill. With these three services implemented, it was important to understand the effects of each of the processes.

On a questionnaire, a sample of participants was asked to allocate percentages to each of these services. The participants were provided the amount of increase in recycling (a fact), and were asked to indicate if other factors had affected this increase, in addition to the three approaches. Only a few other factors were mentioned. Table 9.1 shows the response from one participant. In the example, the participant allocates 60 percent of the improvement to the awareness program and has a level of confidence in the estimate of 80 percent.

The confidence percentage is multiplied by the estimate to produce a usable project value of 48 percent. This adjusted percentage is then multiplied by the actual amount of the improvement in

TABLE 9.1

Example of One Participant's Estimate of Impact

Fact: Recycling volume has increased by 50%			
Factor That Influenced Improvement	Percentage of Improvement Caused By Project	Confidence Expressed as a Percent	Adjusted Percent of Improvement Caused By Project
Green awareness	60%	80%	48%
Convenience for participation	15%	70%	10.5%
Discounts for participating	20%	80%	16%
Other	5%	60%	3%
Total	100%		

recycling volume (post-project minus pre-project value) to isolate the portion attributed to the project. For example, if volume increased by 50 percent, 24 percent would be attributed to the awareness program. The adjusted improvement is now ready for conversion to monetary value and ultimately, for use in the ROI calculation if desired. Although the reported contribution is an estimate, this approach offers considerable accuracy and credibility.

Five adjustments are effectively applied to the participant's estimate to reflect a conservative approach:

◆ Participants who do not provide usable data are assumed to have experienced no improvements.

◆ Extreme data and incomplete, unrealistic, and unsupported claims are omitted from the analysis, although they may be included in the "other" benefits category.

◆ For short-term programs, it is assumed that no benefits from the program are realized after the first year of full implementation. (For long-term programs, additional years may be used.)

◆ The improvement amount is adjusted by the amount directly related to program, expressed as a percentage.

◆ The confidence estimate, expressed as a percentage, is multiplied by the improvement value to reduce the amount of the improvement for the potential error.

When presented to senior management, the result of an impact study is usually perceived to be an understatement of the program's success. The data and the process are considered credible and accurate. As an added enhancement to this method, the next level of management above the participants may be asked to review and approve the estimates from participants.

When using participants' estimates to measure impact, several assumptions are made:

◆ The project encompasses a variety of different activities, practices, and tasks all focused on improving the performance of one or more business measures.

- One or more business measures were identified prior to the project and have been monitored since the implementation process. Data monitoring has revealed an improvement in the business measure.
- There is a need to associate the project with a specific amount of performance improvement and determine the business impact.

Given these assumptions, the participants can specify the results linked to the project and provide data necessary to develop the ROI. This can be accomplished using a focus group, an interview, or a questionnaire.

Using Focus Groups: The focus group works extremely well for this challenge if the group size is relatively small—in the eight to 12 range. Focus groups provide the opportunity for members to share information equally, avoiding domination by any one individual. The process taps the input, creativity, and reactions of the entire group.

The meeting should take about one hour (slightly more if multiple factors affect the results or multiple business measures need to be discussed). The facilitator should be neutral to the process (that is, the program leader should not conduct this focus group). Focus group facilitation and input must be objective. The task is to link the results of the program to business performance. The group is presented with the improvement, and they provide input to isolate the effects of the program.

This approach provides a credible way to isolate the effects of a program when other methods will not work. It is often regarded as the low-cost solution to the issue because it takes only a few focus groups and a small amount of time to arrive at this conclusion.

Using Questionnaires and Interviews: Sometimes, focus groups are not available or are considered unacceptable for the use of data collection. The participants may not be available for a group meeting or the focus groups may become too expensive. In these situations, collecting similar information via a questionnaire or

STEP **9**

The following steps are recommended to obtain the most credible value for program impact:

1. *Explain the task.* The task of the focus group meeting is outlined. Participants should understand that performance has improved. While many factors could have contributed to the improvement, this group must determine how much of the improvement was related to the program.

2. *Discuss the rules.* Each participant should be encouraged to provide input, limiting his or her comments to two minutes (or less) for any specific issue. Comments are confidential and will not be linked to a specific individual.

3. *Explain the importance of the process.* The participants' role in the process is critical. Because it is their performance that has improved, the participants are in the best position to indicate what has caused this improvement; they are the experts in this determination. Without quality input, the contribution of this program (or any other processes) may never be known.

4. *Select the first measure and show the improvement.* Using actual data, the facilitator should show the level of performance prior to and following program implementation; in essence, the change in business results is reported.

5. *Identify the different factors that have contributed to the performance.* Using input from experts—others who are knowledgeable about the improvements—the facilitator should identify the factors that have influenced the improvement (for example, the volume of work has changed, a new system has been implemented, or technology has been enhanced). If these are known, they are listed as the factors that may have contributed to the performance improvement.

6. *Ask the group to identify other factors that have contributed to the performance.* In some situations, only the participants know other influencing factors, and those factors should be identified at this time.

7. *Discuss the link.* Taking each factor one at a time, the participants individually describe the link between that factor and the business results. For example, for the program influence, the participants would describe how the program has driven the actual improvement by providing examples, anecdotes, and other supporting evidence. Participants may require some prompting to provide

comments. If they cannot provide dialogue regarding this issue, chances are good that the factor had no influence.

8. *Repeat the process for each factor.* Each factor is explored until all the participants have discussed the link between all the factors and the business performance improvement. After these links have been discussed, the participants should have a clear understanding of the cause-and-effect relationship between the various factors and the business improvement.

9. *Allocate the improvement.* Participants are asked to allocate the percent of improvement to each of the factors discussed. Participants are provided a pie chart, which represents a total amount of improvement for the measure in question, and are asked to carve up the pie, allocating the percentages to different improvements, with a total of 100 percent. Some participants may feel uncertain with this process, but should be encouraged to complete this step using their best estimates. Uncertainty will be addressed later in the meeting.

10. *Provide a confidence estimate.* The participants are then asked to review the allocation percentages and, for each one, estimate their level of confidence in their estimates. Using a scale of 0 to 100 percent, participants express their level of certainty with their estimates in the previous step. A participant may be more comfortable with some factors than others, so the confidence estimates may vary. These confidence estimates will adjust the results.

11. *Ask participants to multiply the two percentages.* For example, if an individual has allocated 35 percent of the improvement to the program and is 80 percent confident, he or she would multiply 35 percent x 80 percent, which is 28 percent. In essence, the participant is suggesting that at least 28 percent of the team's business improvement is linked to the program. The confidence estimate serves as a conservative discount factor, adjusting for the possible error of the estimate. The pie charts with the calculations are collected without names and the calculations are verified. Another option is to collect pie charts and make the calculations for the participants.

12. *Report results.* If possible, the average of the adjusted values for the group is developed and communicated to them. Also, the summary of all the information should be communicated to the participants as soon as possible. Participants who do not provide information are excluded from the analysis.

interview may be beneficial. With this approach, participants must address the same elements as those addressed in the focus group, but with a series of impact questions on a follow-up questionnaire or in an interview. The questionnaire or interview may focus solely on isolating the effects of the program.

Manager's Estimate of Impact

In lieu of, or in addition to, participant estimates, the participants' manager may be asked to provide input as to the program's influence on improved performance. In some settings, the participants' manager may be more familiar with the other influencing factors. Therefore, he or she may be better equipped to provide impact estimates. The recommended questions to ask managers, after describing the improvement, are similar to those asked of the participants. Manager estimates should also be analyzed in the same manner as participant estimates. To be more conservative, actual estimates may be adjusted by the confidence percentage. When participants' estimates have also been collected, the decision of which estimate to use becomes an issue. If some compelling reason makes leaders think that one estimate is more credible than the other, then the more credible estimate should be used. If they are equally credible, the lowest value should be used with an appropriate explanation.

In some cases, upper management may estimate the percent of improvement attributed to a program. After considering additional factors that could contribute to an improvement—such as technology, procedures, and process changes—management applies a subjective factor to represent the portion of the results that should be attributed to the program. While this is subjective, the input is usually accepted by the individuals who provide or approve funding for the program. Sometimes, their comfort level with the processes used is the most important consideration.

Customer Input on Program Impact

Another helpful approach in some narrowly focused program situations is to solicit input on the impact of programs directly from customers. In these situations, customers are asked why they chose a particular product or service, or asked to explain how their reaction to the product or service has been influenced by individuals or systems involved in the program. This technique often focuses directly on what the program is designed to improve. For example, after implementing a customer service program involving customer response in an electric utility, market research data showed that the percentage of customers who were dissatisfied with response time was reduced by 5 percent when compared to market survey data before the program. Since response time was reduced by the program and no other factor contributed to the reduction, the 5 percent reduction in dissatisfied customers was directly attributed to the program.

Routine customer surveys provide an excellent opportunity to collect input directly from customers concerning their reactions to an assessment of new or improved products, services, processes, or procedures. Pre- and post-data can pinpoint the changes related to an improvement driven by a new program.

When collecting customer input, linking it with the current data collection methods and avoiding the creation of surveys or feedback mechanisms is important. This measurement process should not add to the data collection systems. Customer input could, perhaps, be the most powerful and convincing data if it is complete, accurate, and valid.

Internal or External Expert Input

Internal or external experts can sometimes estimate the portion of results that can be attributed to a program. When using this technique, experts must be carefully selected based on their knowledge

STEP 9

of the process, program, and situation. For example, an expert in the quality of a specific product might be able to provide estimates of how much change in a quality measure can be attributed to a quality training program and how much can be attributed to other factors.

Calculating the Impact of Other Factors

Although not appropriate in all cases, sometimes calculating the impact of factors (other than the program) that influence part of the improvement is possible. In this approach, the program takes credit for improvement that *cannot* be attributed to other factors.

An example will help explain the approach. In a consumer lending training program for a large bank, a significant increase in consumer loan volume was generated after the program was implemented. Part of the increase in volume was attributed to the program, and the remaining was due to the influence of other factors in place during the same time period. Two other factors were identified: 1) an increase in marketing and sales promotion; and 2) falling interest rates.

With regard to the first factor, as marketing and sales promotion increased, so did consumer loan volume. The amount of influence attributed to this factor was estimated using input from several internal experts in the marketing department. For the second factor, industry sources were used to estimate the relationship between increased consumer loan volume and falling interest rates. These two estimates together accounted for a modest percentage of increased consumer loan volume. The remaining improvement was attributed to the program.

This method is appropriate when the other factors are easily identified and the appropriate mechanisms are in place to calculate their impact on the improvement. In some cases, estimating the impact of other factors is just as difficult as estimating the impact of the program, leaving this approach less advantageous. This process can be very credible if the method used to isolate the impact of other factors is also credible.

Use of the Techniques

With all these techniques available to isolate the impact of a program, selecting the most appropriate techniques for a specific program can be difficult. Some techniques are simple and inexpensive, while others are more time-consuming and costly. When attempting to decide, the following factors should be considered:

- ◆ feasibility of the technique
- ◆ accuracy provided with the technique
- ◆ credibility of the technique with the target audience
- ◆ specific cost to implement the technique
- ◆ amount of disruption in normal work activities as the technique is implemented
- ◆ participant, staff, and management time needed for the particular technique.

Multiple techniques or multiple sources for data input should be considered, since two sources are usually better than one. When multiple sources are used, a conservative method is recommended for combining the inputs. The reason is that a conservative approach builds acceptance. The target audience should always be provided with explanations of the process and the subjective factors involved. Multiple sources allow an organization to experiment with different strategies and build confidence with a particular technique. For example, if management is concerned about the accuracy of participants' estimates, a combination of a control group arrangement and participants' estimates could be attempted to verify the accuracy of the estimates.

Final Thoughts

This step presented a variety of techniques for isolating the effects of a program. The techniques represent the most effective

STEP 9

approaches available to address this issue and are used by some of the most progressive organizations. Too often, results are reported and linked with the program without any attempt to isolate the exact portion that can be attributed to it. This issue must be addressed early in the process for all major programs. When accomplished, this step represents the validation of business alignment, pinpointing the actual business results connected to the program.

Report the Results of Business Alignment

Once a program is proven to positively influence business measures, the results must be reported in order to establish the program's validity.

The process of communicating business results must be systematic, timely, and well planned.

With business alignment validated, what's next? Should the results be used to improve the program, change the program design, show the contribution, justify new programs, gain additional support, or build goodwill? How should the data be presented? The worst course of action is to do nothing.

The tenth and final step for successful business alignment focuses on reporting the results of the project. Communicating results is as important as achieving results. Achieving results without communicating them is like planting seeds and failing to fertilize and cultivate the seedlings—the yield simply won't be as prolific. This step provides useful information to help present evaluation data to the various audiences using both oral and written reporting methods.

STEP **10**

The Importance of Communicating Results

Communicating results is critical to the accountability of any type of program. While communicating achieved results to stakeholders after the program is fully implemented is important, early communication is also crucial. Continuous communication ensures that information is flowing so adjustments can be made, and all stakeholders are aware of the issues surrounding the success of the program.

As Mark Twain once said, "Collecting data is like collecting garbage—pretty soon we will have to do something with it." Evaluation data means nothing unless the findings are communicated promptly to the appropriate audiences so they will be aware of the results and can take action if necessary.

The Process for Communicating Results

The process of communicating business results must be systematic, timely, well planned, and represent seven components that should occur in the sequence (shown in Figure 10.1). The first step is one of the most important. It consists of an analysis of the need to communicate results from a program. Possibly, a lack of support for the program was identified, and perhaps the need for making changes to or continuing to fund the program was uncovered. Restoring confidence or building credibility for the program is necessary. Regardless of the triggering events, an important first step is to outline the specific reasons for communicating the results.

The second step focuses on a plan for communication. Planning includes numerous agenda items to be addressed in all communications about the program. Planning covers the actual communication, detailing the specific types of data to be communicated, when, and to which groups.

FIGURE 10.1

The Communication Model for Results

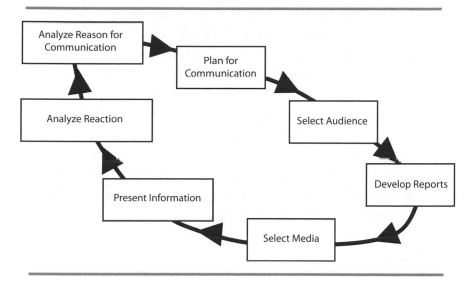

Analyze Reason for Communication → Plan for Communication → Select Audience → Develop Reports → Select Media → Present Information → Analyze Reaction → (Analyze Reason for Communication)

The third step involves selecting the target audiences for communication. Audiences range from top management to past participants, all of whom have their own special communication needs. All groups should be considered in the communication strategy. An artfully crafted, targeted communication may be necessary to win the approval of a specific group.

The fourth step involves developing a report or written material to explain program results. This can include a wide variety of possibilities, from a brief summary of the results to a detailed research report on the evaluation effort. Usually, a complete report is developed. Then, selected parts or summaries from the report are used for different media.

Selecting the medium is the fifth step. Some groups respond more favorably to certain methods of communication. A variety of approaches, both oral and written, are available to the program leaders.

STEP 10

The content and detailed information are presented in the sixth step. The communication is delivered with the utmost care, confidence, and professionalism.

The last step, but not the least significant, is analyzing reactions to the communication. Positive reactions, negative reactions, and a lack of comments are all indicators of how well the information was received and understood. An informal analysis may be appropriate for many situations. For an extensive and more involved communication effort, a formal and structured feedback process may be necessary. Reactions could cause an adjustment to the communication of the same program results to other audiences, or could provide input for adjustments with future evaluation communications. The various steps in the model are discussed further in the next few sections of this chapter.

The Need for Communication

Because there may be other reasons for communicating results, a list should be tailored to the organization and adjusted as necessary. The reasons for communicating results depend on the specific program, the setting, and the unique needs. Some of the most common are:

- ◆ securing approval for the program and allocating resources of time and money
- ◆ gaining support for the program and its objectives
- ◆ securing agreement on the issues, solutions, and resources
- ◆ building credibility for the project team
- ◆ driving action for the improvement of the program
- ◆ showing the complete results of the program
- ◆ underscoring the importance of measuring results
- ◆ motivating prospective participants to be involved in the program
- ◆ demonstrating accountability for expenditures
- ◆ marketing future programs.

Because reasons for communicating results differ, the list should be tailored to each organization.

Planning the Communications

Any successful activity must be carefully planned to produce the maximum results. This is a critical part of communicating the results of the program. Communications planning is important to ensure that each audience receives the proper information at the right time and that appropriate actions are taken. Several issues are important when planning the communication of results:

- What will be communicated?
- When will the data be communicated?
- How will the information be communicated?
- Where will the information be communicated?
- Who will communicate the information?
- Who is the target audience?
- What are the specific actions required or desired?

The communication plan is usually developed early in the project, detailing how specific information is developed and communicated to various groups and the expected actions. In addition, this plan details the timeframes for communication and the appropriate groups to receive the information. The evaluator, key managers, and stakeholders need to agree on the extent of detail in the plan. To communicate appropriately with target audiences, two specific documents should be produced. The first report is a detailed impact study showing the approach, assumptions, methodology, and results. In addition, barriers and enablers are included in the study, along with conclusions and recommendations. The second report should be an eight-page executive summary of the key points, including a one-page overview of the methodology used in the study.

STEP **10**

The Audience for Communications

When approaching a particular audience, the following questions should be asked about each potential group:

◆ Are they interested in the program?

◆ Do they really want to receive the information?

◆ Has a commitment to include them in the communications been made?

◆ Is the timing right for this audience?

◆ Are they familiar with the program?

◆ How do they prefer to have results communicated?

◆ Are they likely to find the results threatening?

◆ Which medium will be most convincing to this group?

For each target audience, three actions are needed. To the greatest extent possible, the program owner should know and understand the target audience. Also, the evaluator should find out what information is needed and why. Each group will have its own desired amount of information. Some want detailed information, while others want brief information. Rely on the input from others to determine the audience needs. Finally, the project team should try to understand audience bias. Each will have a particular bias or opinion. Some will quickly support the results, whereas others may not support them, and others will be neutral. The team should be empathetic and try to understand differing views. With this understanding, communications can be tailored to each group. This is especially critical when the potential exists for the audience to react negatively to the results.

Determining which groups will receive a particular piece of communication deserves careful thought, as problems can arise when one group receives inappropriate information or when another is omitted altogether. A sound basis for proper audience selection is to analyze the reason for the communication, as discussed earlier. Table 10.1 shows common target audiences and the basis for selecting each audience. Several of these stand out as critical. Perhaps the most important audience is the client. This group (or individual) initiates the study, reviews data, and weighs the final

STEP **10**

TABLE 10.1

Common Target Audiences

Reason for Communication	Primary Target Audiences
To secure approval for the results	Client Top executives
To gain support for the program	Immediate managers Team leaders
To secure agreement with the issues	Participants Project team
To build credibility for the team	Top executives
To enhance reinforcement of the program	Immediate managers
To drive action for improvement	Project team
To prepare participants for the program	Immediate managers Participants
To enhance results and quality of future feedback	Participants
To show the complete results of the program	Stakeholders
To underscore the importance of measuring results	Client Project team
To explain techniques used to measure results	Client Project team
To create desire for a participant to be involved	Prospective participants
To demonstrate accountability for expenditures	All employees Shareholders
To market programs	Prospective clients Executives

assessment of the effectiveness of the program. Another important target audience is the top management group. This group is responsible for allocating resources for the program and needs information to help justify expenditures and gauge the effectiveness of the efforts.

Participants need feedback on the overall success of the effort. Some individuals may not have been as successful as others

STEP 10

in achieving the desired results. Communicating the results adds additional pressure to effectively apply the skills and knowledge and improve results in the future. For those achieving excellent results, the communication will serve as reinforcement. Communicating results to participants is often overlooked, with the assumption that, since the study is complete, they do not need to be informed of its success.

Communicating with the participants' immediate managers is essential. In many cases, they must encourage participants to apply skills and knowledge from the program. Also, they support and reinforce the objectives of the program. An appropriate business alignment study improves the commitment to programs and provides credibility for the project team.

The project team must receive information about results. Whether for a brief evaluation or more detailed evaluation studies for which a complete team is involved, those who design, develop, facilitate, and implement the program must be provided information on the program's effectiveness. Evaluation information is necessary so adjustments can be made if the program is not as effective as it should be.

Information Development: The Business Alignment Study

The type of formal evaluation report depends on the extent of detailed information presented to the various target audiences. Brief summaries of results with appropriate charts may be sufficient for some communication efforts. In other situations, particularly with significant programs requiring extensive funding, the amount of detail in the evaluation report is more crucial. A complete and comprehensive impact study report will usually be necessary. This report can then be used as the basis of more streamlined information for specific audiences and various media. The report may contain the sections detailed in Table 10.2.

STEP 10

TABLE 10.2

Format of an Impact Study Report

General Information • Background • Objectives of Study	**Results: Application and Implementation** • Data Sources • Data Summary • Key Issues
Methodology for Impact Study • Levels of Evaluation • Alignment Process • Collecting Data • Isolating the Effects of the Program • Converting Data to Monetary Values (optional)	**Results: Impact** • General Comments • Linkage with Business Measures (Tangible and Intangible) • Key Issues
Data Analysis Issues	**Cost of Program (Optional)**
Results: Reaction and Perceived Value • Data Sources • Data Summary • Key Issues	**Results: ROI and Its Meaning (Optional)** **Barriers and Enablers** • Barriers • Enablers
Results: Learning • Data Sources • Data Summary • Key Issues	**Conclusions and Recommendations** • Conclusions • Recommendations **Exhibits**

While this report is an effective, professional way to present data, several cautions should be followed. Since this document reports the success of a program involving a group of employees (or participants outside the organization), complete credit for the success must go to the participants and their immediate leaders. Their performance generated the success. Another important caution is to avoid boasting about results. Although the methodology is credible, it still has some subjective issues. Huge claims of success can quickly turn off an audience and interfere with the delivery of the desired message.

The methodology should be clearly explained, along with assumptions made in the analysis. The reader should easily see how the values were developed and how the specific steps were followed to make the process more conservative, credible, and accurate. Detailed statistical analyses should be placed in an appendix.

Communication Media Selection

Many options are available to communicate program results. In addition to the impact study report, the most frequently used media are meetings, interim and progress reports, the organization's publications, and case studies. Table 10.3 shows the variety of options.

Meetings

If used properly, meetings are productive opportunities for communicating program results. All organizations have a variety of meetings, and some may provide the proper context for program results. Throughout the chain of command, staff meetings are held to review progress, discuss current problems, and distribute information. These meetings can be an excellent forum for discussing the results achieved in a program when it relates to the group's activities. Results can be sent to executives for use in staff meetings, or a member of the project team can attend the meeting to make the presentation.

Regular meetings with management groups are quite common. Typically, items are discussed that will possibly help their work units. A discussion of a program and the subsequent results can be integrated into the regular meeting format. A few organizations have initiated periodic meetings for all key stakeholders, in which the program leader or evaluator reviews progress and discusses next steps. A few highlights of the program results can be helpful to build interest, commitment, and support for the program going forward.

TABLE 10.3

A Variety of Options for Communicating Results

Detailed Reports	Brief Reports	Electronic Reporting	Mass Publications	Meetings
Impact study	Executive summary	Website	Announcements	Discussions
Case study (internal)	Slide overview	Email	Bulletins	Progress reviews
Case study (external)	One-page summary	Blogs	Newsletters	Quarterly meetings
Major articles	Brochure	Video	Brief Articles	Management group meetings

Routine Communication Tools

To reach a wide audience, internal, routine publications can be used. Whether a newsletter, magazine, newspaper, or electronic file, these types of media usually reach all employees or stakeholders. The information can be quite effective if communicated appropriately. The scope should be limited to general interest articles, announcements, and interviews.

Results communicated through these types of media must be significant enough to arouse general interest. For example, a story with the headline, "Safety project helps produce one million hours without a lost-time accident," will catch the attention of many people because they may have participated in the program and can appreciate the significance of the results. Reports on the accomplishments of a group of participants may not create interest unless the audience relates to the accomplishments.

For many programs, results are achieved weeks or even months after the program is completed. Participants need reinforcement from many sources. If results are communicated to a general audience, additional pressure may exist to continue the program or similar ones in the future.

Stories about participants involved in the program and the results they achieve create a favorable image. Employees are made aware that the organization is investing time and money to improve performance and prepare for the future. This type of story provides information that employees otherwise may not have known and sometimes creates a desire to participate if given the opportunity.

General audience communication can bring recognition to program participants, particularly those who excel in some aspect of the program application and implementation. When participants deliver unusual performance, public recognition can enhance their self-esteem and their desire to continue their excellent performance. Many human interest stories can come from the use of programs. A rigorous program with difficult requirements can provide the basis for an interesting story on participants who made the extra effort to implement what they learned.

Email and Electronic Media

Internal and external web pages on the Internet, company-wide intranets, and email are excellent vehicles for releasing results, promoting ideas, and informing employees and other target groups about results. Email, in particular, provides a virtually instantaneous means with which to communicate and solicit responses from large numbers of people. For major program evaluation, some organizations create blogs to present results and secure reaction, feedback, and suggestions.

Program Brochures and Pamphlets

A brochure might be appropriate for programs conducted on a continuing basis, where participants have produced excellent results.

Also, a brochure may be appropriate when the audience is large and continuously changing. The brochure should be attractive and present a complete description of the program, with a major section devoted to results obtained with previous participants, if available. Measurable results and reactions from participants, or even direct quotes from individuals, could add spice to an otherwise dull brochure.

Case Studies

Case studies represent an effective way to communicate the results of a program. A typical case study describes the situation, provides appropriate background information (including the events that led to the program), presents the techniques and strategies used to develop the study, and highlights the key issues in the program implementation. Case studies tell an interesting story of how the program was implemented and the evaluation was developed, including the problems and concerns identified along the way.

Case studies have value for both internal and external use. The internal use is to build understanding and capability and support internally. Case studies are impressive to hand to a potential client and somewhat convincing for others who are seeking data about the success of programs. Externally, case studies can be used to bring exposure and recognition to the project team and help the organization brand its overall learning function and, in some cases, the organization. A variety of publication outlets are available for case studies—not only in the publications devoted to the functional area, but in general publications as well.

Presenting Information

One of the most important reasons for collecting business results is to provide feedback so that adjustments or changes can be made throughout the program. For most programs, reaction and learning data are routinely collected and quickly communicated to a variety of groups. Sometimes, application and impact data are routinely communicated using a feedback action plan designed to provide information to several audiences using a variety of media. Some of these feedback sessions result in identifying specific actions that need to be taken. This process becomes comprehensive and has to be managed in a very proactive way.

The Presentation of Results to Senior Management

Perhaps one of the most challenging and stressful communications is presenting an impact study to the senior management team, which also serves as the client for the evaluation study. The challenge is convincing this highly skeptical and critical group that outstanding results have been achieved (assuming they have) in a very reasonable timeframe, addressing the salient points, and making sure the managers understand the process. Two particular issues can create challenges. First, if the results are very impressive, making the managers believe the data may be difficult. On the other extreme, if the data are negative, ensuring that managers don't overreact to the negative results and look for someone to blame will be a challenge. Several guidelines can help make sure this process is planned and executed properly.

Plan a face-to-face meeting with senior team members for the first one or two major impact studies. If they are unfamiliar with the ROI methodology, a face-to-face meeting is necessary to make sure they understand the process. The good news is that they will probably attend the meeting because they may not have seen the business results developed for this type of program. The bad news is that it takes a lot of time, usually one hour for this presentation. After a group has had a face-to-face meeting with several presentations, an executive summary may suffice. At this point, they understand the process, so a shortened version may be appropriate. This may involve a one- to two-page summary with charts and graphs showing the six types of measures.

STEP **10**

When making the initial presentation, the results should not be distributed beforehand or even during the session but saved until the end of the session. This will allow enough time to present the process and react to it before the target audience sees the business results. Present the results step-by-step, showing how the data were collected, when they were collected, who provided the data, and how the effect of the program was isolated from other influences. The various assumptions, adjustments, and conservative approaches should be presented so the target audience will begin to buy into the results.

When the data are actually presented, the results are presented one level at a time, starting with reaction and moving through to business results (and as an option, ROI). This presentation allows the audience to see the reaction, learning, application and implementation, and business impact together. Allocate time for each level as appropriate for the audience. This helps overcome the potentially emotional reactions to a very significant or disappointing result.

Show the consequences of additional accuracy if it is an issue. The tradeoff for more accuracy and validity often means more expense. Address this issue whenever necessary, agreeing to add more data if required. Collect concerns, reactions, and issues for the process and make adjustments accordingly for the next presentation.

Collectively, these steps will serve as the basis for planning one of the most critical meetings: the meeting with the program sponsor. Figure 10.2 outlines the approach to this important meeting. Improving communications with this group requires developing an overall strategy and a defined purpose.

Streamlining the Communication

Obviously, executives and management groups will not come to a face-to-face meeting for repeated evaluation studies, nor will they read a complete impact study. Therefore, an executive summary should be used. This represents about a six- to 10-page summary

FIGURE 10.2

Presenting the Impact Study to Executive Sponsors

Purpose of the Meeting	Meeting Ground Rules
• Create awareness and understanding of business alignment. • Build support for the alignment methodology. • Communicate results of study. • Drive improvement from results. • Cultivate effective use of the methodology.	• Do not distribute the business impact study until the end of the meeting. • Be precise and to the point. • Avoid jargon and unfamiliar terms. • Spend less time on the lower levels of evaluation data. • Present the data with a strategy in mind.

Presentation Sequence
1. Describe the program and explain why it is being evaluated.
2. Present the methodology process.
3. Present the reaction and learning data.
4. Present the application data.
5. List the barriers and enablers to success.
6. Address the business impact.
7. Show the method of isolating the effects of this program.
8. Show the costs (optional).
9. Present the ROI (optional).
10. Show the intangibles (separately if ROI data are necessary).
11. Review the credibility of the data.
12. Summarize the conclusions.
13. Present the recommendations for improvement.
14. Discuss next steps.

of the entire report. Still, the process can be further streamlined by considering a one-page summary, as shown in Figure 10.3. This summary, representing an impact study on a leadership program for first-level managers, shows the key data collected. This is the

FIGURE 10.3

One-Page Business Impact Study

Program Title: The Leadership Challenge

Target Audience: First-Level Managers (2000)

Duration: 4 days

RESULTS

Level 1: Reaction	Level 2: Learning	Level 3: Application	Level 4: Impact	Level 5: ROI	Intangible Benefits
Exceeded 4.0 rating except on one measure (3.9 for "provided me with new information")	48% improve- ment in skills or know- ledge	43% of time spent on tasks requiring skills or knowledge	Improve- ments in sales, productivity, costs, and efficiency Total improve- ment: $329,000	105% (Optional)	Job satisfaction Improved teamwork Improved communi- cation

Technique to isolate effects of program: Participant estimates

Technique to convert data to monetary value: Standard values; external experts; participant estimates

Fully-loaded program costs: $160,754 (Optional)

ultimate in efficient communication, but is effective only when the managers understand the different types of data. The audiences must be educated on the methodology so they can understand the streamlined communications. You can use this streamlined commu- nication on a progressive basis, gradually moving managers to this more streamlined method.

Reactions to Communication

The best indicator of how effectively the results of a program have been communicated is the level of future commitment and support from the managers, executives, and sponsors. The allocation of requested resources and strong commitment from top management are tangible evidence of management's positive perception of the results. In addition to this macro-level view, a few techniques can measure the effectiveness of the communication efforts.

Whenever results are communicated, the reaction of the target audiences can be monitored. These reactions may include nonverbal gestures, oral remarks, written comments, or indirect actions that reveal how the communication was received. Usually, when results are presented in a meeting, the presenter will have some indication of how the results were received by the group. The interest and attitudes of the audience can usually be quickly evaluated. Comments about the results—formal or informal—should also be noted and tabulated.

Project team meetings are an excellent arena for discussing the reaction to communicating results. Comments can come from many sources, depending on the particular target audiences. When major program results are communicated, a feedback questionnaire may be used for an entire audience or a sample of the audience. The purpose of this questionnaire is to determine the extent to which the audience understood and/or believed the information presented. This is practical only when the effectiveness of the communication has a significant impact on future actions of the project organizers.

Using Evaluation Data

The principle premise for evaluation is to improve processes—not necessarily to evaluate the performance of a particular group. With process improvement in mind, Figure 10.4 shows some of the typical uses of evaluation data as they relate to the different levels. Many of the uses focus on making the programs better for the future. Others are involved in improving support through reinforcement and commitment for projects and programs.

Someone or some group must be charged with the responsibility of ensuring that these appropriate actions are taken. Sufficient

FIGURE 10.4

Using Evaluation Data

Use of Evaluation Data	Appropriate Level of Data				
	1	2	3	4	5
Adjust program design	√	√			
Improve program	√	√			
Influence application and impact			√	√	
Enhance reinforcement for program			√		
Improve management support for program			√	√	
Improve stakeholder satisfaction			√	√	√
Recognize and reward participants		√	√	√	
Justify or enhance budget				√	√
Reduce costs		√	√	√	√
Market programs	√		√	√	√
Expand implementation to other areas				√	√

effort is rarely focused on this area. Therefore, there is a lack of follow-through. If these ultimate changes or improvements are not made, much of the value of the evaluation is lost. For many programs, particularly those of a comprehensive nature, the original project plan for the evaluation study includes all the steps throughout the process—communicating results, tracking the improvements that must be made, and making adjustments and changes to the program. This ensures that the appropriate use of data does not get left out or that the resources are not applied to it. This is a final piece of the puzzle.

Final Thoughts

The final step in business alignment, communication of results, is a crucial step in the overall alignment process. If this step is not taken seriously, the full impact of the results will not be realized and the alignment efforts may be a waste of time. This chapter begins with the steps for communicating results, which can serve as a guide for any significant communication effort. The various target audiences have been discussed and, because of its importance, emphasis is placed on the executive team. A suggested format for a detailed evaluation report is also provided. Much of the chapter includes a presentation of the most commonly used media for communicating results, including meetings, client publications, and electronic media.

Having business alignment in projects and programs is of the utmost importance. In the current economy, if there is no alignment, there is no funding, which means there is no project. By implementing the 10 steps outlined in this book, and using the V-Model as a guide, business alignment can be achieved successfully and repeatedly.

REFERENCES

Kaufman, Roger, Sivasailam Thiagarajan and Paula MacGillis. (1997). *The Guidebook for Performance Improvement.* San Francisco, CA: Pfeiffer.

Langdon, Danny G. (2000). *Aligning Performance.* San Francisco, CA: Pfeiffer.

Latham, Gary P. (2009). *Becoming the Evidence-Based Manager.* Boston, MA: Brealy.

O'Sullivan, E., G.R. Rassel, and M. Berner. (2008). *Research Methods for Public Administrators.* New York, NY: Pearson Longman.

Phillips, Jack J. and Patricia Pulliam Phillips. (2008). *Beyond Learning Objectives.* Birmingham, AL: ROI Institute.

Phillips, Jack J. and Patricia Pulliam Phillips. (2010). *Measuring for Success: What CEOs Really Think About Learning Investments.* Alexandria, VA: ASTD Press.

Phillips, Jack J. and Patricia Pulliam Phillips. (2004). Return to Sender: Improving Response Rates for Questionnaires and Surveys. *Performance Improvement Journal,* volume 43, number 7. Silver Spring, MD: International Society for Performance Improvement.

Phillips, Jack J. and Patricia Pulliam Phillips. (2007). *Show Me the Money.* San Francisco, CA: Berrett-Koehler.

Phillips, Patricia Pulliam, Jack J. Phillips, and Bruce Aaron. (Forthcoming for 2012). *Survey Basics: A Complete, How-to Guide To Help You Develop Surveys and Questionnaires.* Alexandria, VA: ASTD Press.

Rummler, Geary A. (2004). *Serious Performance Consulting.* Silver Spring, MD: International Society for Performance Improvement.

Business Alignment Examples

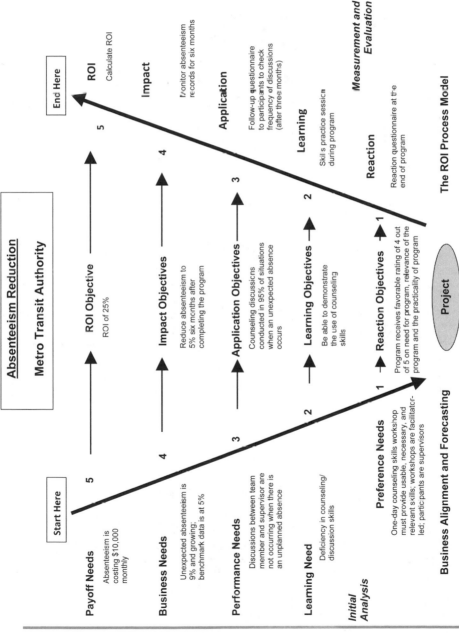

Absenteeism Reduction
Metro Transit Authority

Start Here

5 — **Payoff Needs**
Absenteeism is costing $10,000 monthly

4 — **Business Needs**
Unexpected absenteeism is 9% and growing; benchmark data is at 5%

3 — **Performance Needs**
Discussions between team member and supervisor are not occurring when there is an unplanned absence

2 — **Learning Need**
Deficiency in counseling/ discussion skills

1 — **Preference Needs**
One-day counseling skills workshop must provide usable, necessary, and relevant skills; workshops are facilitator-led; participants are supervisors

Initial Analysis

Business Alignment and Forecasting

End Here

5 — **ROI Objective**
ROI of 25%
ROI
Calculate ROI

4 — **Impact Objectives**
Reduce absenteeism to 5% six months after completing the program
Impact
Monitor absenteeism records for six months

3 — **Application Objectives**
Counseling discussions conducted in 95% of situations when an unexpected absence occurs
Application
Follow-up questionnaire to participants to check frequency of discussions (after three months)

2 — **Learning Objectives**
Be able to demonstrate the use of counseling skills
Learning
Skills practice session during program

1 — **Reaction Objectives**
Program receives favorable rating of 4 out of 5 on need for program, relevance of the program and the practicality of program
Reaction
Reaction questionnaire at the end of program

Measurement and Evaluation

Project

The ROI Process Model

Creating a Green Organization

Level	Needs: Blake Engineering (BE)	Objectives	Evaluation	Level
5	• Help protect the environment. • Save costs.	• Reach ROI target of 10 percent.	• Compare project benefits to costs.	5
4	• Raise image as a green company. • Reduce high energy costs. • Address rising costs of operations. • Address increasing costs of materials/supplies.	• Improve image. • Reduce energy costs. • Reducing materials/supplies • Reducing operating costs.	• Conduct external survey. • Examine organization records.	4
3	• Increase recycling of materials. • Change consumption habits. • Use less materials and supplies. • Start making environmentally friendly choices.	• Six months after the project begins, employees will: –recycle in eight categories –alter consumption patterns –reduce usage, increase conservation –use environmentally friendly supplies.	• Conduct self-assessment questionnaire. • Check the recycle records. • Check records of purchasing eco-friendly products.	3
2	• Determine how actions effect the environment. • Identify specific green methods. • Consider environmental issues.	• All employees will learn: –environmental issues –specific green actions they can take –how to make eco-friendly choices.	• Conduct self-assessment questionnaire. • Conduct environment quiz.	2
1	• Ensure that employees see project as necessary, important, relevant, and feasible.	• Program receives favorable rating of 4 out of 5 on: –necessary to be environmentally friendly –relevant to employees –important to adhering concepts in support of public good.	• Administer reaction questionnaire to all project participants.	1

Farmer Production Program: Global Food Network

Level	Needs	Objectives	Evaluation	Level
5	• Country must produce food for citizens.	• Break even (BCR = 1:1).	• Compare program benefits to program costs.	5
4	• Farmer profits must be positive. • Food quality must meet GFN standards. • Food should be purchased by GFN. • Money must be available.	• Raise farmer profits • Ensure that percent of food meets GFN standards. • Raise GFN purchase to percent of production. • Secure loans for farmers.	• Check farm records. • Check GFN records.	4
3	• Efficient farming methods must be used. • Standards must be followed. • Land must be properly utilized. • Farmers must seek financial assistance.	• Farmers will: – follow standards – utilize land resources – sell food to GFN – apply for low-interest loans.	• Use interviews. • Check action plans. • Distribute questionnaires. • Examine GFN records.	3
2	• Operations equipment finance/accounting • Management • Technology • Loan applications	• Farmers will demonstrate their knowledge of: – operations – equipment utilization – finance/accounting principles – operations management – technology – loan application.	• Prepare a simple quiz. • Offer checklists. • Provide demonstrations. • Promote self-assessment.	2
1	Farmers must see program as: • Feasible • Important to their survival • Relevant to their work • Something they will use	• Program receives favorable rating of 4 out of 5 on feasibility, importance, relevance, and usefulness. • Farmers commit to follow processes.	• Administer reaction questionnaire to farmers.	1

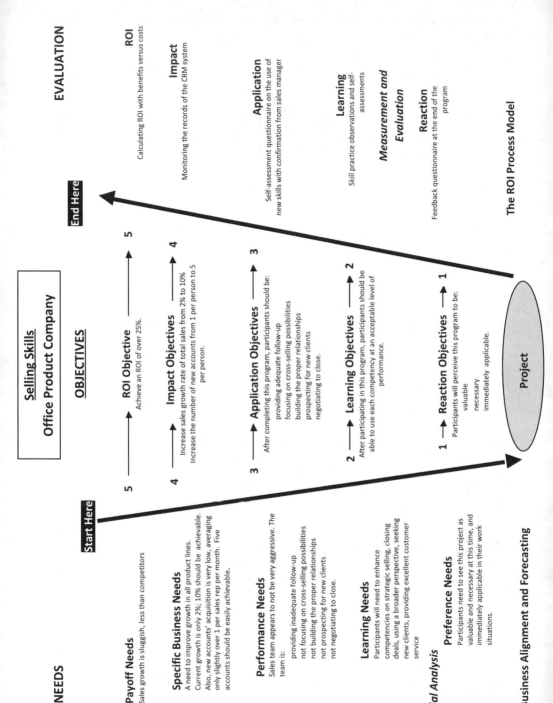

Selling Skills
Office Product Company

NEEDS

Payoff Needs
Sales growth is sluggish, less than competitors

Specific Business Needs
A need to improve growth in all product lines. Current growth is only 2%; 10% should be achievable. Also, new accounts' acquisition is very low, averaging only slightly over 1 per sales rep per month. Five accounts should be easily achievable.

Performance Needs
Sales team appears to not be very aggressive. The team is:

  providing inadequate follow-up
  not focusing on cross-selling possibilities
  not building the proper relationships
  not prospecting for new clients
  not negotiating to close.

Learning Needs
Participants will need to enhance competencies on strategic selling, closing deals, using a broader perspective, seeking new clients, providing excellent customer service

Initial Analysis

Preference Needs
Participants need to see this project as valuable and necessary at this time, and immediately applicable in their work situations.

Business Alignment and Forecasting

OBJECTIVES

5 ← **ROI Objective** → 5
Achieve an ROI of over 25%.

4 ← **Impact Objectives** → 4
Increase sales growth rate of total sales from 2% to 10%
Increase the number of new accounts from 1 per person to 5 per person.

3 → **Application Objectives** → 3
After completing this program, participants should be:
  providing adequate follow-up
  focusing on cross-selling possibilities
  building the proper relationships
  prospecting for new clients
  negotiating to close.

2 → **Learning Objectives** → 2
After participating in this program, participants should be able to use each competency at an acceptable level of performance.

1 → **Reaction Objectives** → 1
Participants will perceive this program to be:
  valuable
  necessary
  immediately applicable.

Project

Start Here

EVALUATION

ROI
Calculating ROI with benefits versus costs

Impact
Monitoring the records of the CRM system

Application
Self-assessment questionnaire on the use of new skills with confirmation from sales manager

Learning
Skill practice observations and self-assessments

Measurement and Evaluation

Reaction
Feedback questionnaire at the end of the program

End Here

The ROI Process Model

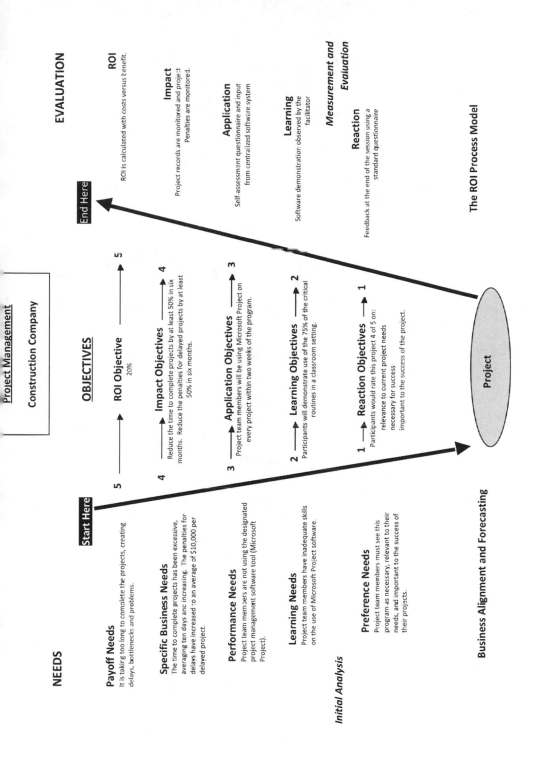

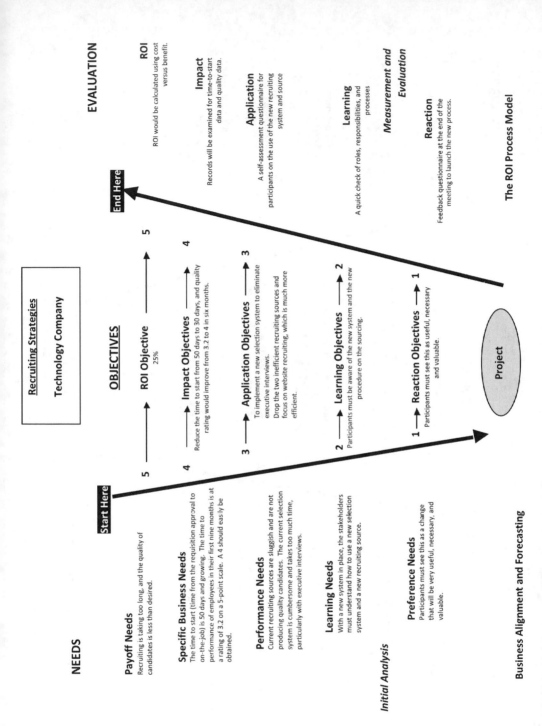

Recruiting Strategies
Technology Company

NEEDS

Payoff Needs
Recruiting is taking too long, and the quality of candidates is less than desired.

Specific Business Needs
The time to start (time from the requisition approval to on-the-job) is 50 days and growing. The time to performance of employees in their first nine months is at a rating of 3.2 on a 5-point scale. A 4 should easily be obtained.

Performance Needs
Current recruiting sources are sluggish and are not producing quality candidates. The current selection system is cumbersome and takes too much time, particularly with executive interviews.

Learning Needs
With a new system in place, the stakeholders must understand how to use a new selection system and a new recruiting source.

Initial Analysis

Preference Needs
Participants must see this as a change that will be very useful, necessary, and valuable.

Business Alignment and Forecasting

OBJECTIVES

ROI Objective
25%

Impact Objectives
Reduce the time to start from 50 days to 30 days, and quality rating would improve from 3.2 to 4 in six months.

Application Objectives
To implement a new selection system to eliminate executive interviews.
Drop the two inefficient recruiting sources and focus on website recruiting, which is much more efficient.

Learning Objectives
Participants must be aware of the new system and the new procedure on the sourcing.

Reaction Objectives
Participants must see this as useful, necessary and valuable.

Project

EVALUATION

ROI
ROI would be calculated using cost versus benefit.

Impact
Records will be examined for time-to-start data and quality data.

Application
A self-assessment questionnaire for participants on the use of the new recruiting system and source

Learning
A quick check of roles, responsibilities, and processes

Measurement and Evaluation

Reaction
Feedback questionnaire at the end of the meeting to launch the new process.

The ROI Process Model

Start Here   5   4   3   2   1

End Here

Quality Project—Pharmaceutical Manufacturer

Level	Needs	Objectives	Evaluation	Level
5	False rejects is a problem. $1.6 million costs due to falsely rejected syringes.	• 25% ROI	• ROI is calculated from: – program costs compared to monetary benefits of program – monetary benefit determined by costs savings of reduced number of false rejects.	5
4	False rejects are defined as syringes rejected when they are actually usable.	• The number of false rejects will be reduced by 10 percent within six months.	• Monitor false rejects for six months • Participant estimates used for isolation	4
3	Inspectors are incorrectly identifying syringes as unacceptable.	• When Implemented, participants should: – follow the five step process during 100% of inspections – utilize job aid as needed – identify barriers to following the five step process.	• Follow-up questionnaire is given to participants to check frequency of skill application and barriers three months after the training. • Unscheduled audits over six months.	3
2	Deficiency in skills to recognize unacceptable syringes.	• Participants must be able to: – understand five step process and job aid – know the difference between acceptable and unacceptable syringes – understand consequences of incorrectly categorizing syringes.	• Demonstrate ability to identify acceptable and unacceptable syringes. • Indicate knowledge and understanding by completing learning assessment.	2
1	One-day workshop and introduction to new job aid. The program must be seen as relevant and important.	• Program receives favorable rating of 4 out of 5 on: – relevance of workshop content and job aid – importance of following the five-step inspection process – intent to use job aid during inspections – other measures important to design and delivery of content.	• Reaction questionnaire is administered at the end of the workshop.	1

Police Project— National Security				
Level	Needs	Objectives	Evaluation	Level
5	• Police officers are contributing to serious problems with the company.	• Break-even (BCR = 1:1)	• Program benefits compared to program costs	5
4	• Crime is too high in four categories. • Citizen complaints about police are excessive.	• In one year: – Crime in four categories will be reduced by ____. – Citizen complaints about police officers will be reduced by ____.	• City records • Country records	4
3	• Police are not following procedures. • Rule of law not followed. • Conflicts are not resolved properly. • Police actions are inconsistent.	• Police officers will: – follow procedures – enforce laws consistently – resolve conflicts.	• Observation • Questionnaire	3
2	• Police have insufficient knowledge about: – legal procedures – rule of law – conflict resolution – communication.	• Police officers will demonstrate knowledge of: – legal procedures – rule of law – conflict resolution – communication.	• Role plays • Demonstrations • Simple quiz • Self assessment	2
1	• Police officers must see this program as: – necessary – helpful – relevant – important to their success.	• Program receives favorable rating of 4 out of 5 on the following measures: – necessary – helpful – relevant – important to their success.	• Reaction questionnaire is administered to police officers.	1

Effective Meetings Program—Global Networks

Level	Needs	Objectives	Evaluation	Level
5	Thousands each month due to excessive, unproductive meetings. Estimated $15,000 per month.	• 25% ROI	• ROI is calculated based on: – program costs including program fee, travel, lodging, meals, facilities, participant time, evaluation costs – monetary benefit determined by time savings from reduction in number of people in meetings, number of meetings, and length of meetings.	5
4	Team spends too much time in meetings. Too many people, too much time, too many meetings.	• Three months after the program, there will be a reduction in cost due to time in meetings as measured by: – reduced number of meetings – reduced number of people in meetings – reduced length of meetings.	• Time in meetings, number of meetings, and number of people in meetings captured by meeting leaders who attended the training. A meeting profile was developed by participants during the workshop and then again three months later in post-training. • Isolating technique is estimation due to the fact that at control groups were not feasible, and time and number of meetings had not been tracked historically.	4
3	Managers and supervisor are not managing their meetings. Too many people attend meetings; no agenda; no follow-up; no structure; no discussion management.	• Upon returning to the job, participants will: – develop a detailed agenda outlining the specific topics to be covered for 100% of meetings – establish meeting ground rules at the beginning of 100% of meetings – use at least 50% of effective meeting techniques in every meeting – follow up on meeting action items within three days following 100% of meetings.	• Follow-up questionnaire administered to participants three months after the program to determine achievement with objectives.	3

Effective Meetings Program—Global Networks (Continued)

2	Managers and supervisor need to develop meeting management skills; learning is important.	During the workshop, participants will demonstrate their ability to: – develop a meeting profile – develop a meeting agenda – select the appropriate participants – manage discussions and conflict – use effective meeting techniques – manage follow-up activities.	• Facilitator assessment of meeting profile • Written test • Skill practice observation	2
1	Two-day workshop with relevant and important content	Program receives favorable rating of 4 out of 5 from 80% of participants on: – content relevance to the job – intent to apply content immediately upon return to job – other measures important to design and delivery of content.	• Reaction questionnaire is administered at the end of the workshop.	1

Work at Home Project—Family Mutual Insurance

	Needs Assessment		Program Objectives		Evaluation	
5	Having employees travel long distances is causing serious costs to the company and damage to the environment.	→	ROI of 25%	→	Calculate the ROI	5
4	• Average commuting time for staff is 1 hour and 44 minutes. • Office expenses are high and increasing. Cost per office space is very high, average $17,000 per employee. • Turnover is high, averaging 22.3%; benchmark data suggest that it should be about 12%. • Productivity needs to improve; the current level has been unchanged in two years. • Absenteeism is excessive at 7%; benchmark data s at 4%. • Stress is high.	→	• Commuting time is reduced to an average of 15 minutes a day. • Office expense is reduced by 20%. • Turnover is reduced to 12%. • Productivity is improved by 5%. • Absenteeism should be reduced. • Stress should be reduced. • Carbon emissions should be reduced. • The company's image as a green company is enhanced. • Employee engagement should improve.	→	• Commute time, office expense, productivity, turnover and absenteeism are monitored in six months. • Questionnaires are administered.	4
3	• Employees will attend briefing session and volunteer to work at home. • Employees must be productive in the home environment, making it free from distractions. • Managers must manage effectively from remote location. • Work-at-home policies will be administered properly.	→	• Managers should conduct a meeting. • At least 30% of employees in the claims processing area will work at home. • Procedures and policies are implemented. • Offices at home are built and equipped to work at home. • Managers will follow the procedure to make sure the process works. • Managers should manage the remote employees effectively.	→	• Follow-up questionnaire is given to employees and managers after three months.	3

Work at Home Project—Family Mutual Insurance (Continued)

2	• Employees need to understand the reality of working at home, the conditions, roles, and regulations. • Employees must have the discipline and the tenacity to work at home. • Mangers must understand how this can work. • Managers must know how to manage remotely.	• Employees must have the discipline and tenacity to work at home. • Employees will know the realities of working at home, the conditions, roles, and regulations. • Managers must know how to explain the policies and regulations for working at home. • Managers must know how to manage remotely.	• Checklist • Questionnaire
1	• Participants must see this offer as satisfying to their jobs, important to their own success and needs, rewarding, and motivational. • Managers must see this as a necessary, appropriate, and important to their own organization's objectives.	• Employees will find satisfaction with, and see the importance of, working at home. • This work arrangement will be rewarding and motivational. • Managers will view this new work arrangement as important and appropriate. • Managers will see the need for the new work arrangement.	• Reaction questionnaire at the end of the meeting to announce the program on the follow-up questionnaire.

I N D E X

I

image, xvi–xvii, 32, 33–34
impact measures/data
   See also program impact
   action plans to collect, 104–108
   performance contracts to
      measure, 108–109
   questionnaires to collect, 109–
      113
   types of, 35–38, 100–101
impact objectives, 69–70
impact study, 142–144, 152–154
improvement plans/guides, 88, 90
information, presenting, 147–151
interviews, 44–45, 127, 130
investment/funding decisions, xvii

J

job aids, 83, 93
job and task analysis, 58

K

knowledge, 66

L

learning
   design for, 83–85
   objectives, 65–66, 67
   sequencing and timing, 85
   style, 83–84
learning needs
   demonstrations, 59
   description of, xxx
   importance of, 55–56
   job and task analysis, 58
   management assessment, 60
   measurement categories, 57–58
   observations, 59
   subject matter experts, 58
   tests, 59–60
life cycles, 2

M

management
   assessment, 60
   design and roles for, 93–97
   estimates, 130
   expectations and, 83
   focus on projects, xxiii

information, presenting to,
   148–149, 150, 151
   support from, xvii, 2–3
meetings, 144
memos, 79
mind mapping, 53

N

nominal group technique, 46–49

O

objectives, xxv–xxvi, xxxi
   application, 66–68
   impact, 69–70
   learning, 65–66, 67
   levels and types of, 64
   power of, 73–75
   reaction, 63–65
   return on investment, 70–72
observations, 59
output, 28, 30

P

Pareto principle, 119
participants
   estimates, 124–130
   role of, 79–81
payoff needs
   costs, 23–24
   description of, xxvii–xxviii
   determining, 8
   identifying, 19–22
   importance of, 17–19
   opportunities, 20–21
   opportunities, not so obvious,
      21–22
   opportunities, value of, 24
performance
   contracts, 91–92, 108–109
   learning objective, 66
   measurements, 99–102
   measurements, converting to
      usable ones, 103–104
   monitoring, 102–104
performance needs
   affinity diagrams, 53
   analysis techniques, 41–42
   brainstorming, 50–51
   cause-and-effect (fishbone)
      diagram, 51–52

The ROI Institute, Inc. is the leading resource on research, training, and networking for practitioners of the Phillips ROI Methodoloqy.

With a combined 50 years experience in measuring and evaluating training, human resources, technology, and quality programs and initiatives, founders and owners Jack J. Phillips, PhD, and Patti P. Phillips, PhD, are the leading experts in return-on-investment (ROI).

The ROI Institute, founded in 1992, is a service-driven organization that strives to assist professionals in improving their programs and processes through the use of the ROI Methodology. Developed by Jack Phillips, this methodology is a critical tool for measuring and evaluating programs in 18 different applications in more than 40 countries.

The ROI Institute offers a variety of consulting services, learning opportunities, and publications. In addition, it conducts internal research activities for the organization, other enterprises, public sector entities, industries, and interest groups. Together with their team, Jack and Patti Phillips serve private and public sector organizations globally.

Build Capability in the ROI Methodology

The ROI Institute offers a variety of workshops to help you build capability in the ROI Methodology. Among the many workshops offered through the ROI Institute are:

- One-day *Bottomline on ROI* Workshop—provides the perfect introduction to all levels of measurement, including the most sophisticated level, ROI. Learn the key principles of the Phillips ROI Methodology and determine whether your organization is ready to implement the process.
- Two-day *ROI Competency Building* Workshop—the standard ROI Workshop on measurement and evaluation, this two-day program involves discussion of the ROI Methodology process, including data collection, isolation methods, data conversion, and more.

ROI Certification™

The ROI Institute is the only organization offering certification in the ROI Methodology. Through the ROI Certification process, you can build expertise in implementing ROI evaluation and sustaining the measurement and evaluation process in your organization. Receive personalized coaching while conducting an impact study. When competencies in the ROI Methodology have been demonstrated, certification is awarded. There is not another process that provides access to the same level of expertise as our ROI Certification. To date, over 5,000 individuals have participated in this process.

For more information on these and other workshops, learning opportunities, consulting, and research, please visit us on the web at www.roiinstitute.net, or call us at 205.678.8101.

A B O U T   T H E   A U T H O R S

Jack J. Phillips is a world-renowned expert on accountability, measurement, and evaluation. Phillips provides consulting services for Fortune 500 companies and major global organizations. The author or editor of more than 75 books, he conducts workshops and presents at conferences throughout the world.

Phillips has received several awards for his books and work. On two occasions, *Meeting News* named him one of the 25 Most Influential People in the Meetings and Events Industry, based on his work on ROI. The Society for Human Resource Management presented him an award for one of his books and honored a Phillips ROI study with its highest award for creativity. The American Society for Training and Development gave him its highest award, Distinguished Contribution to Workplace Learning and Development for his work on ROI. His work has been featured in the *Wall Street Journal, BusinessWeek,* and *Fortune* magazine. He has been interviewed by several television programs, including CNN.

His expertise in measurement and evaluation is based on more than 27 years of corporate experience in the aerospace, textile, metals, construction materials, and banking industries. Phillips has served as training and development manager at two Fortune 500 firms, as senior human resource officer at two firms, as president of a regional bank, and as management professor at a major state university.

This background led Phillips to develop the ROI Methodology revolutionary process that provides bottom-line figures and accountability for all types of learning, performance improvement, human resources, technology, and public policy programs. Phillips regularly consults with clients in manufacturing, service, and government organizations in over 50 countries in North and South America, Europe, Africa, Australia, and Asia.

Phillips has undergraduate degrees in electrical engineering, physics, and mathematics; a master's degree in Decision Sciences from Georgia State University; and a PhD in Human Resource Management from the University of Alabama. He has served on the boards of several private businesses—including two NASDAQ companies—and several nonprofits and associations, including the American Society for Training and Development, International Society for Performance Improvement, and the National Management Association. He is chairman of the ROI Institute, Inc., and can be reached at (205) 678-8101, or by email at jack@roiinstitute.net.

Patti P. Phillips is president and CEO of the ROI Institute, Inc., the leading source of ROI competency building, implementation support, networking, and research. A renowned expert in measurement and evaluation, she helps organizations implement the ROI Methodology in countries around the world, including South Africa, Australia, Chile, Brazil, Romania, Ireland, Canada, and the United States.

Since 1997, following a 13-year career in the electric utility industry, Phillips has embraced the ROI Methodology by committing herself to on-going research and practice. To this end, she has implemented ROI in private sector and public sector organizations. She has conducted ROI impact studies on programs such as leadership development, sales, new-hire orientation, human performance improvement, K-12 educator development, and educators' National

Board Certification mentoring. Her current work includes research and application of the ROI Methodology in workforce development, community development, and social sector programs.

Phillips teaches others to implement the ROI Methodology through the ROI Certification™ process, as a facilitator for ASTD's ROI and Measuring and Evaluating Learning Workshops, and as adjunct professor for graduate-level evaluation courses. She serves on numerous doctoral dissertation committees, assisting students as they develop their own research on measurement, evaluation, and ROI.

Phillips speaks on the topic of ROI and accountability at conferences and symposia in countries around the world. She is often heard over the Internet as she presents the ROI Methodology to a wide variety of audiences via webcasts.

Phillips's academic accomplishments include a PhD in International Development and a master's degree in Public and Private Management. She is certified in ROI evaluation and has been awarded the designations of Certified Professional in Learning and Performance and Certified Performance Technologist. She can be reached at (205) 678-8101 or by email at patti@roiinstitute.net.

The Phillips serve as authors and editors for a variety of publications. Their most recent publications include: *Measuring ROI in Learning & Development: Case Studies from Global Organizations* (ASTD, 2012), *Measuring the Success of Coaching* (ASTD, 2012), and *Measuring Leadership Development: Quantify Your Program's Impact and ROI on Organizational Performance* (McGraw-Hill, 2012). Other books recently authored by the Phillips include *The Green Scorecard: Measuring the ROI in Sustainability Initiatives* (Nicholas Brealey, 2011); *Return on Investment in Meetings and Events: Tools and Techniques to Measure the Success of All Types of Meetings and Events* (Elsevier, 2008); *Show Me the Money: How to Determine ROI in People, Projects, and Programs* (Berrett-Koehler, 2007); *The Value of Learning* (Pfeiffer, 2007); *Return on Investment Basics* (ASTD, 2005); and *Proving the Value of HR: How and Why to Measure ROI* (SHRM, 2005), among many others.

THE *ASTD* MISSION:

Empower professionals to develop knowledge and skills successfully.

The American Society for Training & Development provides world-class professional development opportunities, content, networking, and resources for workplace learning and performance professionals.

Dedicated to helping members increase their relevance, enhance their skills, and align learning to business results, ASTD sets the standard for best practices within the profession.

The society is recognized for shaping global discussions on workforce development and providing the tools to demonstrate the impact of learning on the organizational bottom line. ASTD represents the profession's interests to corporate executives, policy makers, academic leaders, small business owners, and consultants through world-class content, convening opportunities, professional development, and awards and recognition.

Resources
- *T+D (Training + Development)* Magazine
- ASTD Press
- Industry Newsletters
- Research and Benchmarking
- Representation to Policy Makers

Networking
- Local Chapters
- Online Communities
- ASTD Connect
- Benchmarking Forum
- Learning Executives Network

Professional Development
- Certificate Programs
- Conferences and Workshops
- Online Learning
- CPLP™ Certification Through the ASTD Certification Institute
- Career Center and Job Bank

Awards and Best Practices
- ASTD BEST Awards
- Excellence in Practice Awards
- E-Learning Courseware Certification (ECC) Through the ASTD Certification Institute

Learn more about ASTD at www.astd.org.
1.800.628.2783 (U.S.) or 1.703.683.8100
customercare@astd.org

031130.62220